Avgusta Udartsev

Easy Saxophone
for Beginners

Theory, Practice and 55 Songs.
For Kids 12+ and Adults.
With Online Video and Audio

The saxophone photo on the cover and p. 9; p. 17; p. 30; p. 31 - © horiyan / istockphoto
Picture design p. 1 - © Daniel Oravec / depositphotos
Picture design p. 12 - © Amati Kraslice / Collage by Gisbert König, from Wikimedia Commons
Photo p. 13 - © 3345557 / Pixabay
Photo p. 18 - © Şevval Karataş / Pexels
Picture design p. 41; p. 89; p. 117; p. 161 - © brgfx / Freepik

For any questions, comments or suggestions, email us at:
avgustaudartseva@gmail.com

CONTENTS

Chapter 3 - *Part 1*

Chapter 2 - *Part 2*

Chapter 3 - *Part 2*

Welcome to the World of Saxophone!

The saxophone is a monophonic[1] instrument. Its sound is often compared to the human voice. It is a very expressive and fascinating instrument associated with jazz, intricate harmonies and vivid emotions. True, it is a complex instrument in terms of its design, but it has a very attractive, velvety sound. Picking up saxophone is not as difficult as you would imagine. Trust me, it is truly a fascinating process! Moreover, it would be impossible to imagine jazz without this instrument.

In this book you will learn everything you need to know about the saxophone: its types, its various parts, holding it and the specifics of sound production. In fact, the information presented in this book will be useful not only for the purpose of learning to play the saxophone but will also introduce you to music in general.

We have also prepared 55 songs that will help you master the instrument with joy and learn to read notes. We have also included basic music theory and technical exercises that will help you get a sense and master the jazz style of playing the instrument. Classical and jazz melodies are selected according to the particular task of mastering the instrument step-by-step. The book includes songs with lyrics for practicing correct sound production and phrasing. The accompaniment to the 20 songs is suitable for soprano, alto, tenor and baritone saxophone. This way you get the opportunity to master playing the saxophone with accompaniment and, who knows, maybe it will inspire you to create your own musical group one day!

I hope that this book will help you get a sense of all the features of saxophone playing so that you can play this amazing instrument to your full enjoyment.

Best of luck!

Avgusta Udartseva

---

[1] An instrument is considered monophonic if it can play only one note at a time.

Chapter 1

About Saxophone

For any questions, comments or suggestions, email us at:
avgustaudartseva@gmail.com

1. What is a Saxophone?

The saxophone (often referred to colloquially as the "sax") is a type of single-reed woodwind instrument with a conical body usually made of brass. It was invented by the Belgian musical instrument maker Adolphe Sax in the early 1840s and patented on June 28, 1846.

In terms of sound production it belongs to the family of reed woodwind musical instruments. Although the saxophone is made of metal (silver, brass and other metals, but most frequently brass), it is still traditionally designated as part of the woodwinds. It is similar in construction to the clarinet, its shape reminiscent of the bass clarinet.

The saxophone is used in a wide variety of musical styles, including classical, jazz (such as big bands and jazz ensembles), and contemporary music. The saxophone is also used both as a solo/lead melody instrument or as a member of the brass section in some styles of rock and roll and pop music.

The saxophone is one of the main instruments in jazz and related genres, as well as pop music. The instrument has a full and powerful sound, a smooth tone, and great technical possibilities.

The Saxophone Family

SOPRANO **ALTO** **TENOR** **BARITONE**

There are two pitch types of modern saxophones: B♭ (B-flat) and E♭ (E-flat).

Soprano, alto, tenor and baritone saxophones are the most commonly used saxophones.

Type of saxophone	Pitch
Soprillo (Sopranissimo)	B♭
Sopranino	E♭
SOPRANO	B♭
ALTO	E♭
TENOR	B♭
BARITONE	E♭
Bass	B♭
Contrabass	E♭
Subcontrabass	B♭

This book is written primarily for alto saxophone but you can just as well use it to learn a different saxophone type. The fingering is the same, the only difference is the size of the instrument and its pitch. The book has an appendix of audio tracks to 20 songs. These accompaniments are presented in two keys: if it says "Sax E♭", then this accompaniment is suitable for all instruments in the E♭ scale (Sopranino, Alto, Baritone, Contrabass). If it says "Sax Bb", then the accompaniment is suitable for all instruments in the B♭ scale (Soprillo (Sopranissimo), Soprano, Tenor, Bass).

The Meaning of Saxophone Key

There is a difference between a written note for a saxophone and the note that sounds on the tuner. For example, a C note on an Alto saxophone would be E-flat on a piano (or the tuner).

The tenor saxophone's pitch is B♭ (B-flat), therefore the C note will correspond to B-flat on the piano.

Where would You See a Saxophone Played?

Nowadays, it is common to see an alto or tenor saxophone in a city brass band. As you may know, brass bands accompany various traditional festivals or other big city events or often play before a soccer or football game.

Some schools have brass bands where students learn to play saxophone and often perform in the orchestra or as soloists at school events.

2. Saxophone and Jazz

At the end of the 19th century a new musical style called jazz was born in the US and the saxophone almost immediately became one of its feature instruments. The specific sound of the instrument and its enormous expressive possibilities suited this style very well.

Well-established mass production of these instruments contributed to their rapid spread. The earliest surviving records of jazz musicians of the late 1910s - early 1920s prove that the saxophone enjoyed great popularity within this genre of music.

In the swing era (from the mid-1930s) there was a widespread proliferation of jazz orchestras (or "big bands"), in which the presence of the saxophone group became standard. As a rule, such an orchestra had at least five saxophones (two altos, two tenors and one baritone). Sometimes the composition could vary and the saxophonist could also double as a clarinet or flute player.

Famous Saxophone Players

In modern jazz the saxophone remains one of the primary instruments. Each saxophone player has his own style, his own music, and some players have left a bright mark in the history of music.

Charles (Charlie) "Bird" Parker, Jr., (1920-1955) was an American jazz saxophonist and composer, one of the founders of the bebop style.

Charlie Parker, along with Louis Armstrong and Duke Ellington, is considered one of the most influential musicians in the history of jazz.

In 2005, Henry Selmer Paris' saxophone manufacturing company introduced a special "Tribute to Bird" series of alto saxophones to commemorate the 50th anniversary of Charlie's death (1955-2005).

Ben Webster (March 27, 1909, Kansas City, Missouri - September 20, 1973, Amsterdam, Netherlands) was an American jazz musician, tenor saxophonist, and a prominent swing performer.

Lester Young (full name Lester Willis Young, 1909 - 1959) was an American tenor saxophonist and clarinetist, one of the greatest musicians of the swing era.

Coleman "Hawk" Hawkins (1904 - 1969, New York) - American jazz musician, one of the famous tenor saxophonists, who created his own performing school.

John William Coltrane (1926-1967) - American jazz saxophonist. His album "A Love Supreme" is considered by many to be a masterpiece.

Michael Leonard Brecker (1949 – 2007, New York City) was an American jazz musician, tenor saxophonist, and composer.

Jay Barnett Bekenstein (born May 14, 1951) is an American saxophonist and composer.

Kenny Garrett (born October 9, 1960) is an American jazz musician, saxophonist, and flutist.

Eric Marienthal (1957-present) is a saxophonist who plays a mix of styles (modern jazz, smooth jazz, fusion and pop). Marienthal has also written instruction books, including Comprehensive Jazz Studies & Exercises, The Ultimate Jazz Play Along, and The Music of Eric Marienthal.

Theodore Walter "Sonny" Rollins, (September 7, 1930) is an American jazz musician, saxophonist, composer, and bandleader.

Among others are Julian "Cannonball" Adderley (1928-1975), Gerry Mulligan, Michael Brecker, Phil Woods, Stan Getz, Paul Desmond, and so on.

Which Saxophone should I Choose?

The alto saxophone is one of the most popular wind instruments and the most popular in the saxophone family. It would be better to start training on this saxophone among all the other varieties. It is the best option for beginners, children and adults, amateurs and professionals in terms of size, sound production, sound versatility and dimensions.

In terms of size it is neither too small or too big. In terms of tone it is the most optimal and universal. In the lower register it can sound like a tenor and in the upper range it can sound like a soprano. Of course, much depends on the skill of the performer, the reed, mouthpiece and the manner of playing.

If you are ready to buy a new instrument, you can choose a student version from brands such as Yamaha, Amati, Weltklang, Yanagisawa, Selmer, Roy Benson. Perhaps a cheaper instrument may seem like high quality at first glance, but over time you may experience serious problems with the operation of the mechanisms or the pads on the inside of the keys may come off. Since the instruments of reputable manufacturers have already proved themselves, often buying even a second-hand instrument from Weltklang or Amati could be a good and reliable choice when compared to an instrument of an unknown manufacturer. In any case, when buying a saxophone, you should carefully check the instrument, look at how it is packed, whether it sits tightly in the case or whether there is a plastic plug closing the opening of the main part of the saxophone.

If you decide to buy a used instrument but doubt its quality, you can check it for mechanical defects by contacting a saxophone repairman. Perhaps music schools and music stores can tell you where to find a reliable saxophone repair shop. In most cases, used instruments look and function quite well. As a rule, they are sold by folks who have something to do with saxophones and music. Perhaps they are musicians who have bought a more suitable instrument for themselves.

Some saxophone repairmen may also sell instruments. Usually, they restore them and then put them up for sale.

To sum up, when buying a used instrument, you should pay attention to the seller. Be sure to talk to him or her. He should know the history of the instrument he is selling, its features and character. Try to find out as much as possible. The more detailed and open will be your dialog with the seller, the more confident you can feel about the instrument. Ideally, if possible, ask the seller to make a video for you or perhaps the seller can play the instrument on offer. Then you know you can play it too, even if a little later when you learn.

If you are not just looking for a saxophone as a learning instrument, but see it as a musical partner and friend, you will inevitably find it and recognize it!

3. The Anatomy of a Saxophone

The saxophone is a conical tube usually made of special alloys: tombac (an alloy of copper and zinc), paktong (the same composition, with nickel added) or brass. To make it more compact, the saxophone tube is curved. In soprano saxophones, due to the short length of the instrument, the neck is usually upright.

The saxophone consists of three main body parts: the mouthpiece, the body, and the neck. The mouthpiece, which is very similar to the clarinet mouthpiece, is also beak-shaped, made of black ebonite or plastic, and sometimes of metal.

The saxophone is equipped with a complex system of valves that close and open the holes on its body to adjust the pitch. The holes are covered by leather pads attached to the keys, which are pressed by the player.

The number of valves varies from 19 to 22 depending on the instrument.

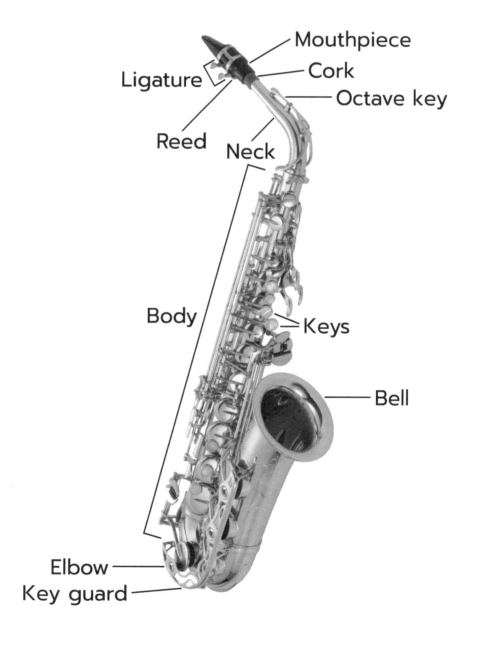

Modern musical instrument manufacturers sometimes produce straight alto saxophones and, conversely, curved soprano saxophones.

The top of the saxophone has a place to attach a note stand. If you will be playing in an outdoor orchestra, this is handy to use so you don't have to memorize a huge amount of notes.

4. Before You Start Playing: Putting the Saxophone Together

Check for all the necessary parts:

1. The mouthpiece.
2. The reed (reed strength of 2 or 2.5 will work for beginning students).
3. The ligature.
4. The mouthpiece cap.
5. The neck (top part of the instrument).
6. The body.
7. The neck strap (for alto and larger saxophones).
8. The cork grease.
9. Protective mouthpiece patches (needed to prevent your teeth from slipping on the mouthpiece; it is not necessary but highly recommended).
10. Saxophone stand (optional).
11. Music stand (if you plan to use sheet music).

Watch the video[1]

Saxophone stand

When you buy the instrument, it comes in a special case in which it can be easily stored and transported. All the parts mentioned above are already included in the kit, except for the protective mouthpiece, the cleaning cloth needed to clean the inside and outside of the instrument, the saxophone stand and the music stand. You can choose and buy these items separately according to your taste.

The reeds are expendable and are also bought separately. There might be just one reed per package. Depending on the number and duration of lessons, the reed will wear out or may be damaged accidentally, so you should have several reeds handy, preferably of different strength so you can work on your tone using a stronger reed (#3), and sometimes if you need to play for a long time, you can play using a reed with a smaller number (#2, #2,5). The lifespan of a single reed can be 1 month or longer.

Although the saxophone outfit should include a mouthpiece that is more universal in sound, often musicians will choose a different mouthpiece, individually, depending on the goals that they choose for themselves. Some people like a softer sound, while others like a bolder and brighter sound.

---

[1] See page 42 for all videos, PDF and audio files.

The Saxophone Assembly Order

A brief step-by-step outline:

1. Take the short tube (neck) that has a thin layer of cork on it and apply a thin layer of cork grease over it.

2. Put the mouthpiece (turning it slightly) over the neck tip covering about 3/4 of the neck cork.

3. Take the reed out of the case (plastic packaging), soak the tip in water or take it gently into the mouth to make it moist. Place the reed under the mouthpiece, covering the opening, without moving it sideways, so that the thin part of the reed does not go beyond the border of the mouthpiece and is reflected under the mouthpiece (this part will be touching the lower lip). With experience and practice you will get better and better at this. Eventually you will learn to set the reed perfectly straight.

4. Carefully put on the ligature being careful not to damage the reed (the thin part of the reed is very delicate). You can put the ligature on first and then insert the thick part of the reed. Tighten the screws and check the stability of the reed in this position. Make sure that the reed does not move when tightening the ligature.

5. After inserting the reed, protect it with the cap and carefully put it on without touching the thin part of the reed.

6. Now take hold of the bell of the main part of the instrument (body) and loosen the screw at the top of the instrument. Remove the plastic plug that covers the main instrument opening. The plug is needed when storing the saxophone in the case. To ensure that the neck (small tube) can be put on easily, be sure to apply some lubricant to the connecting part between the neck and the main part of the instrument (body). Attach the neck so that the mouthpiece is on the opposite side of the bell.

7. Slide the neck strap (required for alto and larger instruments) over your head and around your neck.

8. Connect the hook from the neck strap to the ring on the saxophone, adjusting its length and helping remove the strain off the right thumb that supports the instrument.

Watch the video

The saxophone assembly order

Important! Since the walls of the saxophone are thin, do not use excessive force at any time when assembling and cleaning the saxophone.

5. Caring for Your Instrument

Wipe your instrument inside each time after playing. Dampen the pads with special paper to remove any residual moisture. Before placing your saxophone in the case, insert the plastic plug into the instrument. Wipe the case and the mechanisms of the instrument to remove any fingerprints.

Remove the reed and use a cloth to clean the inside of the mouthpiece.

Also clean the neck and base of the instrument.

To avoid damaging the tip of the mouthpiece, do not pull the rag completely through it. Always keep the rag clean and dry.

Always put the instrument back in its case when you have finished playing. When doing so, make sure there is nothing in the case that can damage its keys. Do not hold on to the keys during assembly. Always keep a close eye on the instrument.

It is essential to observe strict hygiene by washing the mouthpiece and reed well at least once a week under a stream of <u>cool</u> running water directly under the tap, without using detergents or brushes.

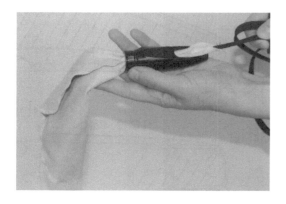

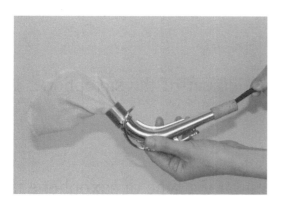

Saxophone Parts that Need Special Attention

The mouthpiece is a very important element of the saxophone. It is where the air is collected before being directed into the saxophone. The reed is attached to the mouthpiece. Mouthpieces differ in material and shape. The shape determines the angle at which the sound enters the saxophone and the force with which you need to tense the facial muscles.

The variety of genres and styles where the saxophone is being used has determined a large number of variations in the structure of the mouthpiece, depending on the desired sound.

Mouthpieces, like reeds, are differentiated by numbers. The higher the number, the harder it is to play.

There are mouthpieces with Baffle (bridge). Such mouthpieces have more directed sound. They are used more often in modern music. Mouthpieces without the baffle have a brighter sound. They are more universal.

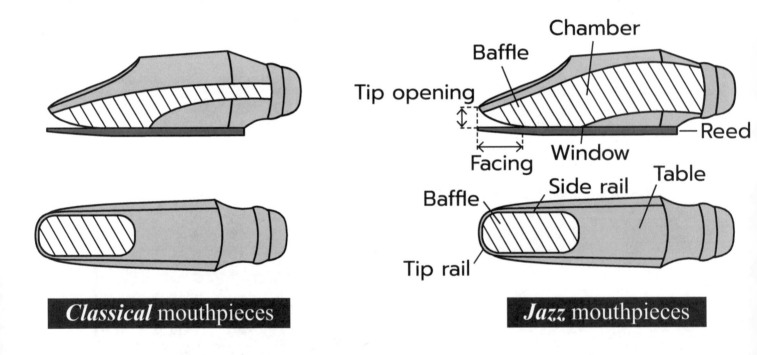

Classical mouthpieces

Jazz mouthpieces

The reed (tongue) is the sound-producing element of the saxophone. It is also similar in structure to the clarinet reed.

It is usually made of bamboo or cane.

The reeds come in different sizes, depending on the type of saxophone they are designed for. For example, a tenor saxophone reed is slightly longer than an alto saxophone reed. The reed can be thinner or thicker in the thin part of the reed. The thicker the thin part is, the more difficult it is to blow. In turn, the sound becomes more rounded and deeper. For beginners, it is recommended to play using a #2 or #2.5 reed.

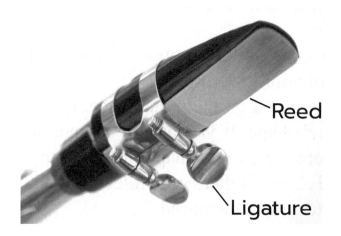

Watch the video

Placing the reed on the mouthpiece

The reed is attached to the mouthpiece using a special device called **a ligature,** which is essentially a small clamp with two screws. Sometimes the screws are tightened from the top of the mouthpiece, but in most cases from the bottom. The ligature also has an effect on the sound. Its shape and material can change the way the instrument sounds.

The ligature for the classical saxophone is made of metal, while jazz and other genres of musicians use leather ligatures along with metal ones, which give the reed a freer oscillation.

To protect the reed from accidental damage, a special metal or plastic **cap** is used, which is put on the mouthpiece when the instrument is not used for a long time or during short breaks between playing.

The Specifics of Playing Position. Embouchure

The word *embouchure* comes from the French word "bouche" meaning "mouth", and defines the way a saxophonist tenses the facial muscles and positions the lips when playing the saxophone.

The embouchure is perhaps the most controversial element of learning to play the saxophone. The fact is that a vast number of musicians use completely different ways of positioning their lips. In other words, they have different embouchure. This means that it doesn't really matter how you put your lips together or what kind of embouchure you have. All that matters is what result you are getting.

If you are getting a good sound, who cares how you place your lips on the mouthpiece? However, there are some fundamental things you need to know about the embouchure to achieve a particular sound.

1. The most important thing to know is the position of your teeth on the mouthpiece and the position of your lower lip.
2. The two front upper teeth are placed on the mouthpiece. It is important that the front teeth are in good shape. If you have a chipped tooth, you should see a dentist and restore the correct shape of the tooth. Take the mouthpiece in your hands. It is better if there is a protective sticker on top of the mouthpiece where the teeth will be placed.

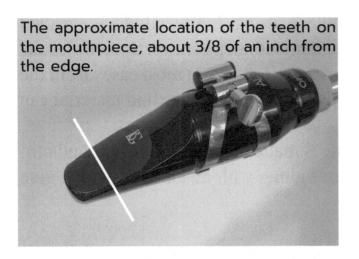
The approximate location of the teeth on the mouthpiece, about 3/8 of an inch from the edge.

The protective sticker on the mouthpiece is designed to prevent the teeth from slipping on the mouthpiece. The stickers are available in clear or black. Choose one to suit your taste.

Place your upper teeth on the mouthpiece less than half an inch (1 cm) from its edge. The distance from the edge of the mouthpiece is selected individually. Where the teeth should be placed depends on:
• the bite;
• the thickness of the lips of the player;
• the shape of the mouthpiece;
• other factors.

How Deep should the Teeth be Placed on the Mouthpiece?

1. The teeth are placed at the very edge of the mouthpiece. In this case saxophone players might say: "taking less mouthpiece". In this case, the sound of the saxophone is soft, cotton-like. Such a sound is not suitable for playing. It is a frequent mistake of beginning saxophonists.
2. If you put your teeth far from the edge - "taking more mouthpiece" - you get a sharp, loud and uncontrolled sound.
3. If you put your teeth in an intermediate position between these two extremes, you will get a relatively correct sound.

The Most Important Part about Embouchure

After the upper teeth are placed on the patch there comes the most important moment in the embouchure - **the placement of the lower lip.**

The lower lip is placed close to the lower teeth, but not wrapped around the teeth. It should stop just above the lower teeth, as if resting on the teeth with its inner part. The lips form something like a rubber ring, which covers the mouthpiece from all sides. This is similar to the position of the lips when whistling.

One way to find out the correct position of the lower lip on any one mouthpiece is the "business card" method.

Slip a business card between the reed and the body of the mouthpiece. The lower lip should be where the business card stops.

With the lower lip in this position, the reed in your mouth is in the best position for playing. That is, the edge of the reed is in a free state and can vibrate. In this way, it will be possible to push the reed with the lower lip and thus regulate the sound of the saxophone.

Important Reminder!

The work of the facial muscles determines the sound of the saxophone.

The main part of the saxophone is the reed, so the attention should be directed to the reed when you're getting ready to play. The most important thing in the work of all the muscles of the saxophonist is that the reed vibrates freely and nothing interferes with it.

To help the reed vibrate freely, you need to:
1. Open your mouth
2. Relax the muscles of the lower jaw
3. Tense the chin muscles slightly.

In this case, the lower lip will rest on the teeth and become elastic like a spring. You can check this by touching it with your finger. If done correctly, the reed will be on a soft, elastic "spring" and will vibrate freely. When playing, the cheeks should not puff up!

Try practicing the embouchure in front of a mirror.

⊠ If your chin goes up, then you are not doing it correctly.

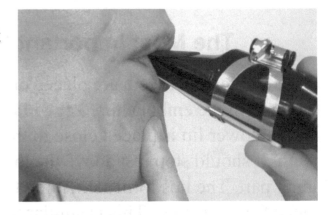

☑ The chin should form a sort of a spatula and be sufficiently extended.

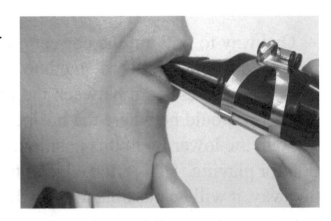

Now attach the mouthpiece to the neck (with a rotating motion) and blow into this small "trumpet". Try to start the sound by lightly striking your tongue against the reed, imitating the word "Too"!

Try to achieve an even, long sound (without pushing breaths), take breaks for 1-2 minutes if the muscles of the face and lip get tired. You need to get used to it and feel how the sound is born! When playing, keep your larynx as open as possible, just like when yawning. Save the air that is blown into the mouthpiece. If you feel dizzy from hyperventilation, you may want to pause for a while.

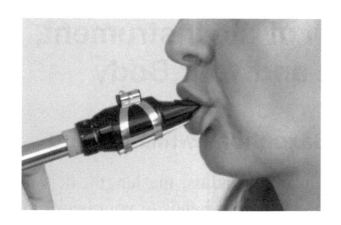

☒ Incorrect position.
Lips turned out

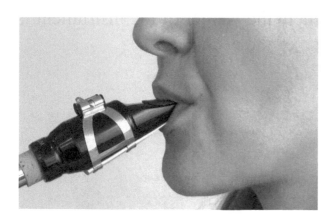

☑ Correct position.

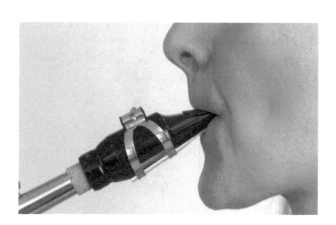

☒ Incorrect position.
Lips tucked

27

6. The Position of the Instrument, Your Arms and Your Body

How to Hold the Saxophone while Playing

Place the neck strap over your head and adjust the length. It is needed to transfer the weight of the saxophone from your hands to your neck (1).

There is another kind of strap where the weight of the instrument is distributed evenly, on the shoulders instead of the neck (2).

(1)

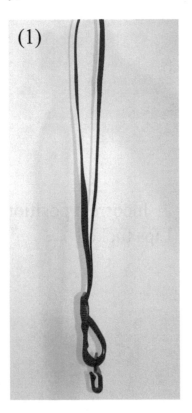

(2)

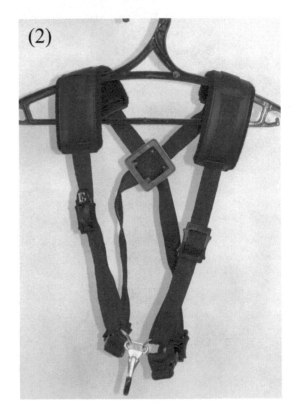

About halfway on the saxophone body there is a metal ring used to attach the instrument with a carabiner hook found on your strap.

The ring is an important part of the instrument, although it does not affect the sound itself.

The metal hook must be rubber coated, otherwise, if it comes into contact with your instrument, it will cause wear and tear, and the ring may break while the instrument is in use. At the same time, the plastic hook is not so reliable and

may crack, causing a drop, which can lead to the breaking of the mechanisms or deformation of the body of the instrument. Some musicians use a rope and make a small ring from a strong cord. Such a link-mediator between the metal hook and the ring will protect the saxophone ring from wear and tear and possible breakage.

To sum it up, it is recommended to use a special strap that has a metal carabiner with a rubber coating.

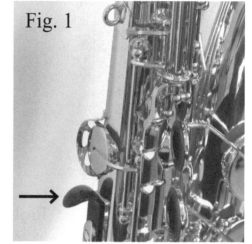

Fig. 1

The saxophone is supported by the thumbs. The thumb of the right hand is placed under the hook at the bottom of the saxophone body (Fig. 1).

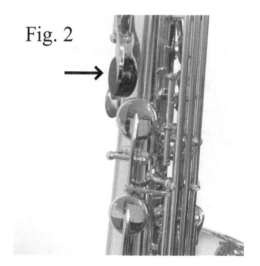

Fig. 2

The thumb of the left hand is placed on a support - a pad in the upper part of the body (Fig. 2).

This creates three points of support for the saxophone:

1. Neck strap - the main support for the saxophone while playing;

2. Right thumb - supports the saxophone from below;

3. Left thumb - adjusts the position of the instrument in relation to the saxophonist's body.

Placement of the Fingers on the Saxophone

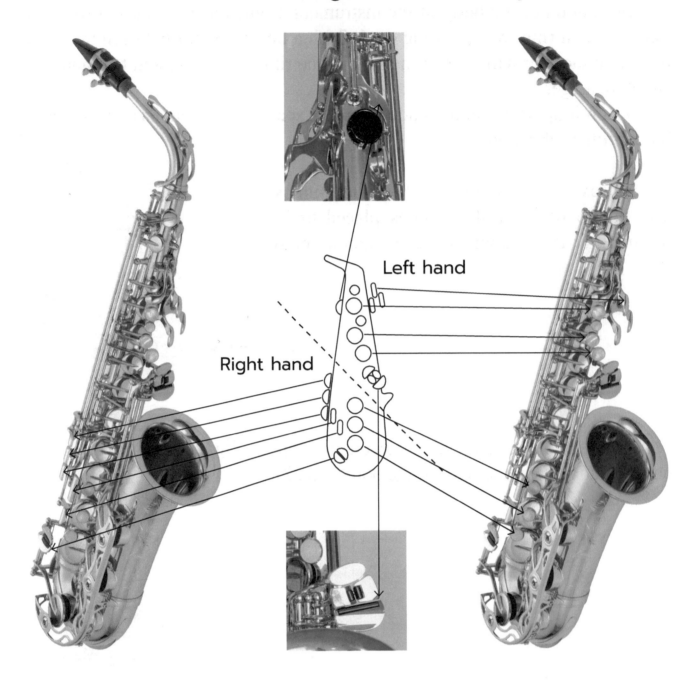

The placement of your fingers on a musical instrument to produce musical sounds is called fingering. You will learn the entire fingering of the saxophone on page 86 (see page 88 for printing). For now, we will only discuss the initial position of the fingers. This is the prep position before pressing the keys.

The fingers are placed on the main (mother-of-pearl) keys, about half an inch away from the surface or resting on them without actually pressing the keys.

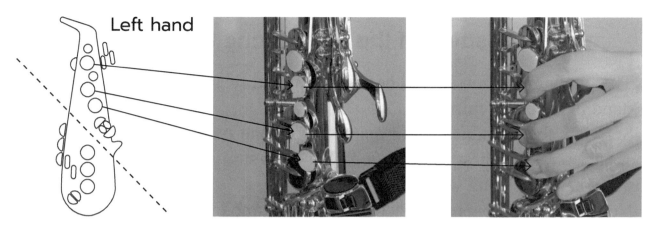

Left hand: The index, middle, and ring fingers rest on the large round keys. These keys are located at the top of the case. The little finger of the left hand is not yet engaged, but there is also a key for it, an auxiliary key. The thumb of the left hand is placed on a thumb rest - a special pad in the upper part of the body. Next to left thumb rest there is an octave key. The thumb is placed on the pad to make it convenient to press the octave key. The small round key and the topmost key (sometimes it is also present and can be in the form of a mother-of-pearl coating on some saxophone models) remain free.

Right hand: The index, middle, and the ring fingers are placed on the round keys at the bottom of the case. The little finger is not yet engaged. The fingers of the hand placed on the saxophone should not be straight. The fingers should be slightly rounded in shape as if you were holding a small apple. Avoid "backward bending" of the fingers in the first phalanx, as this contributes to excessive tension in the muscles and negatively affects the mobility and rhythmic movements of the fingers. Touch the keys without excessive pressure and slightly before the sound emerges. To ensure accurate finger movements, use fine wrist movements when pressing the side valves with your index fingers. Press the keys of the saxophone with the pads of your fingers, i.e., the tips of your fingers should be exactly above the keys of the saxophone. It is possible to take your fingers off the keys of the saxophone when playing, the main thing is to hit the desired key in time.

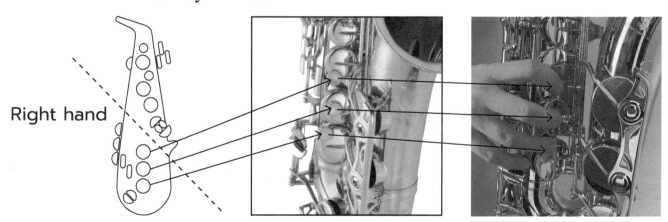

Position of the Saxophone Player

The playing position should be as natural and relaxed as possible. It is best to stand in front of a mirror.

Set your feet shoulder width apart, saxophone hanging on the neck strap, your back straight, chest straightened, shoulders straightened, arms in a relaxed position hanging along your body.

Now, raise your arms and place your right thumb on the hook designed for it (Page 29; Fig. 1). Don't stick it in too far!

The fingers are relaxed and in a natural half-bent state. Avoid any excessive arm flexion at the wrists. The wrist should form a straight line with the forearm. Some flexion of the left wrist is allowed while touching the side flaps with the fingers of the left hand.

There is an adjustment screw on the right thumb hook. With the screw you can change the position of the hook and achieve the correct (perpendicular) position of the ring finger, but this is not necessary if you are comfortable.

Place the thumb of the left hand on the thumb rest (Page 29; Fig. 2) The very tip of the left thumb should slightly overhang the octave key key, so that at the right moment you can press or release the key without lifting the left thumb off the thumb rest.

Your head should remain straight, chin slightly lowered. The saxophone is directly in front of you, while slightly tilted relative to the body - the lower part of the instrument is slightly to the right compared to the upper part and directed to the right hip. At the very beginning of your training, the saxophone should rest against the front of your right thigh with the protection valve located at the back of the saxophone under the thumb hook of your right hand - this will give the instrument a more stable position. The saxophone should not sag past the saxophonist's body.

To find the correct position of the neck lean forward slightly so that the instrument hangs on the strap directly in front of you. You do not need to point the saxophone into the correct position with your hands, it should hang freely on the strap. Now use your thumbs to pull the saxophone away from you and straight in front of you. The weight of the saxophone should rest entirely on the strap, the thumbs should only deflect the instrument away from the saxophonist's body.

The neck should be turned in such a way relative to the saxophone body so that the mouthpiece is pointed exactly at the mouth. The correct position of the neck is centered on the relationship between the positions of the octave key pin (1), located on the very top of the saxophone body, and the neck's stiffening plate (2), which is located on its back side.

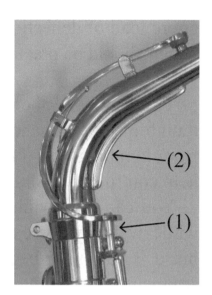

The horizontal position of the mouthpiece pad, on which the upper teeth are placed, is set not relative to the saxophone, but relative to the floor, so that the saxophonist's head is in a naturally level position, not tilted to the left. That is, the platform of the mouthpiece on which we place the upper teeth should be parallel to the surface of the floor of the room.

You must not reach for the mouthpiece! The strap should be adjusted so that when your head is in a straight position, the mouthpiece of the saxophone is directly under your lower lip. To get the mouthpiece in the playing position, you should open your mouth, slightly lower your chin, tilt your head forward and bring the saxophone closer to you. At the same time, you should never move your head forward, but only tilt it slightly, keeping the position relative to the spine. Accordingly, it is not the head that moves towards the mouthpiece, but the saxophone is moved towards the player and the mouthpiece takes its position in the mouth.

When you have mastered it enough and your skill level allows you to move the saxophone naturally during playing and move it away from the body, the entire load of deflection should be on the tendon of the thumb, the muscles of which should be practically relaxed.

The weight of the instrument should never be placed on the thumb. The thumb of the left hand limits the movement of the saxophone and prevents it from bumping your face with the mouthpiece. Thus, the thumbs should only help control the position of the instrument.

You can play while sitting, standing (even while walking, for example in an orchestra), but it is easier for beginners to master the instrument while sitting. Solo saxophonists usually play standing on stage. So, you will need to learn to be able to play both sitting and standing! Sitting is easier because you are less tired and can spend more time practicing.

In order to play while sitting, you should sit on the front edge of a chair. Avoid comfortable chairs with armrests since it is difficult to maintain good posture in them. Get a stiffer chair, such as a kitchen chair.

In no case should you recline on the backrest if you have one. The saxophonist's body should be upright. Feet should not be tucked underneath you, not pulled forward. Knees should be bent at an angle of 90 degrees. The position is stable, the saxophone is in front of you, everything else is the same as when playing while standing.

7. Playing Your First Sounds! Proper Breathing

Before you start playing an assembled instrument, I suggest that you first try blowing into the mouthpiece alone (with the reed attached to it!). Good posture is important to learn in the first stages of learning any instrument. Study the information in this chapter carefully and get started.

It is important to realize that if a beginner saxophonist uses a wrong technique of sound production, wrong breathing and hand placement when working on sound and technique, the more he practices, the more he will solidify his mistakes, from which he will not easily get rid of.

Important point: If you do not know how to make the right start while playing, go to the mirror. Look at yourself. Inhale. Did your shoulders go up? Then the breathing in is incorrect. Exhale. Try taking a breath with your stomach. The stomach should inflate, and the shoulders and chest should remain in place. You've got it!

Your goal is to create a clean, consistent sound when you blow into the mouthpiece. At first, practice blowing without pressing any keys. Don't puff up your cheeks or raise your shoulders when you take a breath. This develops bad habits and makes it difficult to maintain an even tone.

If you blow too hard, you will produce a harsh, unpleasant sound. Try blowing more gently to create a more melodious sound. Depending on the tune, the breath can be fast or slow, but always deep and using stomach muscles. That said, try not to draw in air using your chest. This will impede exhaling and make you lose all the air much quicker.

You should be able to produce a sustained note for about half a minute. If you cannot, you are blowing too hard. It should be noted that there is a cause and effect relationship between the note (sound) and the force with which you blow into the instrument.

How to Tongue a Note

There are two basic ways to start playing a note on the saxophone: air attack and tongue attack. You can start playing a note simply by blowing into the saxophone. The force of the airflow will cause the reed to vibrate, and the instrument will produce a sound.

Tongue attack is when you use your tongue to start the sound more precisely. Both methods are used in saxophone playing.

The overall goal is to start playing each note using a quality, stable sound. Starting to play long notes with a tongue attack can cause a change in your embouchure. When practicing playing long notes, it is better to use the air attack. You need to practice getting a consistent tone throughout the entire note. You can also use your tongue to stop the flow of air by touching the reed with your tongue. Or you can leave the sound to fade without using the tongue to stop the air. It's important to realize that the tongue doesn't create the sound. It is the force of the airflow that makes the reed vibrate that creates the sound. And the tongue's job is to let air into or shut off the instrument.

Imagine that your airflow is water from a hose with a constant pressure and your tongue is a faucet. You would have to turn the water on first before the water begins to flow. The same way, air pressure must be created before the saxophone produces a sound.

At first, without an instrument, practice just blowing out some air. Then without stopping close your mouth with your tongue (like using a cork in a bottle) but keep the airflow pressurized since the air is not getting out. This can be compared to pressurized water in a hose that has been temporarily shut off with a faucet. As soon as you remove your tongue from the top of your mouth, the airflow will resume its exit at the same rate because the air pressure has not been stopped.

You can do the same with the mouthpiece. Gently place your tongue on the reed and start increasing the air pressure in the back of your tongue. As soon as you release your tongue, the sound will appear.

To make it easier to understand how the tongue works, you can pronounce the syllable "Too" without using your voice. Some people pronounce the syllable "dah". It is not that important which syllable you choose. What is important is to pronounce the letter "t" clearly. Why the letter "t"?

This way the tongue prevents the air from going straight into the mouthpiece and a clear beginning of the sound occurs. Only when you see in the music a curved line called a slur which connects the notes, only then do you not separate the notes from each other with your tongue or do it very carefully. The melody will sound smooth and one sound will flow smoothly into another. But in this case, you should pay attention to the finger articulation, so that your fingers are deft and rise up in time, otherwise the transition from one note to another will not be so precise.

Ending Your Note

As with the beginning of the sound, there are **soft and hard** withdrawals. Soft ending is performed without the tongue, i.e., only with the help of weakening and stopping the breath. Hard release of sound is performed with the tongue, i.e. the tongue works as a valve blocking the access of air to the mouthpiece of the instrument, and also as a damper, i.e., forcibly suppressing the vibrations of the saxophone reed, thus creating a sharp end of sound.

The Position of the Tongue while Playing a Note

As you start to learn to play the saxophone, you will just blow into the mouthpiece with enough force to make the reed vibrate and create a sound, but as you progress you will want to "pronounce" the note with your tongue because this will give you a nice clean beginning of the note and a nice, clean ending to it.

There are different ways in which you can position your tongue and move it to pronounce a note with your tongue, but the technique and method chosen will depend on several factors. Undoubtedly everyone's tongue is different in size just as everyone's mouth is different so everyone chooses a mouthpiece individually that they are comfortable with.

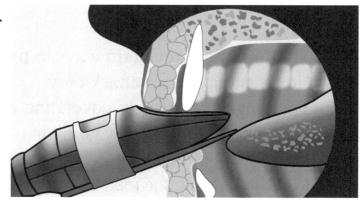

Let's consider the variations of tongue positioning for pronouncing a note that are commonly used.

Touching the reed with the tip of the tongue while the rest of the tongue does not move. You place the tip of your tongue just under the tip of the reed so it doesn't vibrate and make sure it is close to the tip of the reed so there are no squeaks. Then start blowing to create some air pressure. Then release the tip of your tongue, which will cause the reed to immediately start vibrating and making a sound. To stop the sound, you place the tip of your tongue back on the reed in the same position, which will stop the reed vibration and stop the sound. The space inside your mouth remains almost the same and this allows you to play notes at a fast tempo. This helps create a cleaner beginning and end of notes. Note that the airflow is constantly going through the instrument and the tongue is only used to stop the vibration of the reed, not to stop the airflow.

The second way of touching the reed with the tongue is tighter and <u>the tongue closes the airflow to the mouthpiece</u> and the note sounds sharper.

We are touching the reed with the tip of the tongue (1). You need to experiment with how much pressure to apply to the reed.

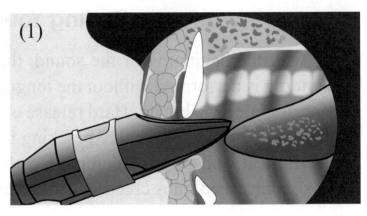

(1)

You can also choose the second position of the tongue (2) - when the tip of the tongue is placed at the bottom of the teeth and raised so that it touches the reed a little further (roughly about half an inch). In the same way the tongue touches the tip of the reed so that it doesn't vibrate. Then you create air pressure, and when you're ready, you release your tongue so that the reed starts to vibrate.

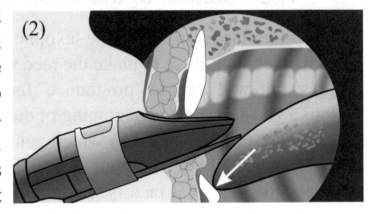

(2)

To sum up, the three main ways to produce the sound are:
1. No tongue, using air attack only.
2. The tongue completely covers the entrance to the mouthpiece blocking the sound and the airflow going in (two variations of tongue placement at the moment of blocking the sound).
3. Lightly touching the reed with the tongue to only stop the vibration of the reed without blocking the airflow. In this case, the role of the tongue is to stop the sound without stopping the air flow.

Watch the video

How to tongue
a note

Tuning the Instrument

All saxophone types share a difference between the sound of a written note and the actual note sounded according to the generally accepted pitch (A = 440 Hz), which is indicated by a device called *a tuner* and commonly known as "Concert C pitch". Even the piano (acoustic), over time begins to change its tuning and it must be re-tuned by by a piano tuning professional, who also uses a tuner, as this device indicates the correct pitch of the concert C or concert A note. The A note on the tuner has a vibration frequency of 440 Hz. This sound serves as the tuning starting point for all acoustic instruments.

To tune the instrument before playing with accompaniment or in an ensemble with other instruments, you should **play the C note on the Alto saxophone.** You should listen to the note so that you adjust it to the rest into in a unison while the tuner displays **the E♭ (E-flat) note.** The difference of 3 semitones is an interval called a "minor 3rd". You will learn about intervals later in this book.

Any note on an alto saxophone will be lower by a minor 3rd relative to a tuner or piano. For example, if you were to play an A note on an Alto saxophone, you will hear a C on a tuner, or if you play a G note, you will hear a B-flat on a tuner (▶).

Tenor and soprano saxophone have a different interval difference between the music notation and the actual sound. When playing the C, it will correspond to a B-flat on the tuner.

The note will not always match the tuner. In this case there is a method of more accurate tuning. **The saxophone is tuned by adjusting the position of the mouthpiece on the neck.** If you hear that the notes sound slightly lower than the accompaniment of the song and it sounds out of tune, you need to raise the pitch by slightly pushing (twisting) the mouthpiece in, and vice versa – pulling the mouthpiece out will lower the pitch. The degree of lip pressure on the reed can also affect the pitch of the note. Try not to squeeze the reed with your lower lip and choose a comfortable sounding position.

Higher pitch ⟵ ⟶ Lower pitch

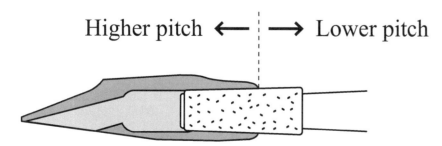

Page 39

Saxophone type	Saxophone pitch	Tuner / piano pitch
Alto	C A	E♭ (E-flat) C
Tenor / Soprano	C	B♭

To sum up, first you play a note on the instrument and then play a note on the tuner. You can also install the app "Tuner by Piascore" or any other tuning app on your phone.

Chapter 2
Part 1

Theory and Practice

All Videos (Playlist)

All videos are included in the same playlist on YouTube *(online):*

or use the link:

cutt.ly/6eoFrwNU

All Audios and PDF Files for Downloading

All of the audio  and PDF files are also available on Google Drive:

or use the link:

cutt.ly/WeoFtNDZ

1. Important! Be sure to download all files from Google Drive to your computer. We did have a glitch in our system once and our files were temporarily unavailable online. It would be best to download them all at once so you have offline access to them anytime.

2. In songs with accompaniment in audio files marked with "+" sign you will hear an example of how to play the melody (saxophone plays the melody). The audio files marked with "-" have no melody, just the accompaniment track. It is there for you to play along with the track.

For any questions, comments or suggestions, email us at:
avgustaudartseva@gmail.com

42

Introduction to Part 1

It is certainly not enough to know how to press the keys on the saxophone. Likewise, it is important to understand and read written music. To achieve this you need to acquire musical literacy, which is not that difficult. After learning the basic theory you can then use it to play not just the saxophone, but literally any other instrument!

The world of music will be open to you and you will be able to read melodies that are familiar to you and that you like so much.

Not only will your repertoire increase, but you will also be able to record your own music should you come up with a unique melody in a moment of inspiration.

This book contains different songs and melodies that are easy to play. Some songs have lyrics making it easier to understand the structure of musical phrases and help you play more expressively.

1. The Stave, Notes and Treble Clef

Music is written on a set of 5 lines called **a Stave** (Staff[1]). The two clefs that are most commonly used are **the Treble clef** and **the Bass clef.**

Music notes are oval-shaped symbols that are placed on the lines or in spaces between them. They represent musical sounds called **pitches.**

The lines of the stave are numbered from bottom to top (1-5). The spaces between the lines are also numbered from bottom to top (1-4). If the notes appear higher on the stave, they sound higher in pitch. If the notes appear lower on the stave, they sound lower in pitch.

The Treble clef

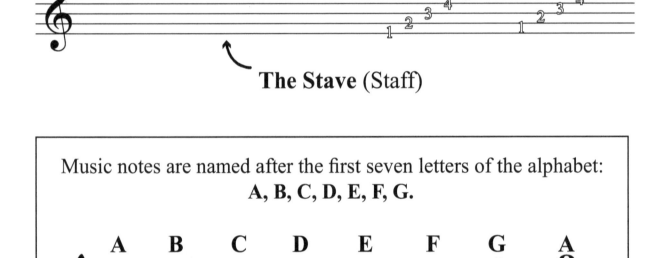

The Stave (Staff)

Music notes are named after the first seven letters of the alphabet:
A, B, C, D, E, F, G.

---

[1]Words "stave" and "staff" carry the same meaning referring to the five horizontal lines and four spaces between them used for music notation. The term "staff" is more common in the US while "stave" is more often used in Britain. In this book we use the term "stave".

In the treble clef the names of the notes on the lines from bottom to top are **E, G, B, D, F.**

Notes on the Line

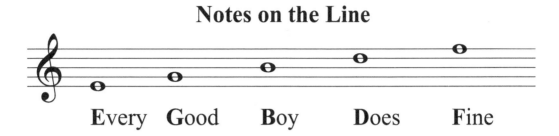

Every   Good   Boy   Does   Fine

Notes in the Spaces

The names of the notes in the spaces from bottom to top spell **FACE.**

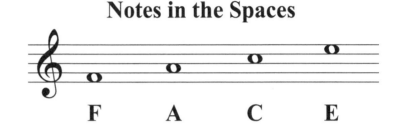

F   A   C   E

Ledger lines are those little lines with notes on them that appear above or below a musical stave.

The purpose of these lines is to extend the stave in both directions, up and down.

An octave is simply the distance between one note and that same note repeated in the next higher or lower register within the audible range.

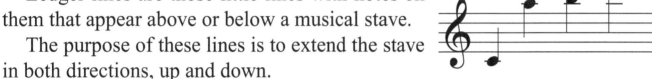

1st Octave   2nd Octave

We see that the notes are repeated (7 notes in total). The same note up an octave sounds exactly the same but higher.

Stems extend downward on the left side when the note appears on or above the 3rd line of the stave. Stems extend upward on the right side when the note appears below the 3rd line of the stave.

Stems Up   Stems Down

2. Note Values

While the placement of notes on the stave indicates the pitch, the duration of the note (how long the note is held down) is determined by the value of the note.

A Whole note is drawn as an open oval.

A whole note is equal to four counts (or beats). Count and clap the rhythm evenly (hands together for 4 beats). The beat numbers are written under the notes. Also, say "ta-ah-ah-ah" (in a continuous sound) and clap.

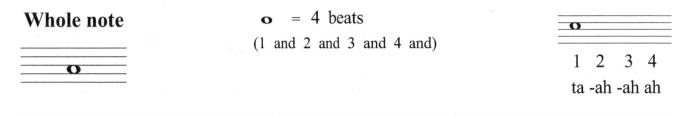

Two Half notes equal the duration of one whole note.

A half note is equal to two counts (or beats). Count and clap the rhythm evenly (holding your hands together for 2 beats). The beat numbers are written under the notes. Also, say "ta-ah" (in a continuous sound) and clap.

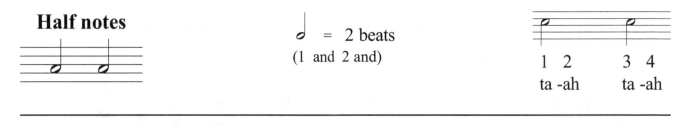

Four Quarter notes equal the duration of one whole note.

A quarter note is equal to one count (or beat). Count (1, 2, 3, 4) and clap the rhythm evenly (once per beat). The beat numbers are written under the notes. Also, say "ta" and clap.

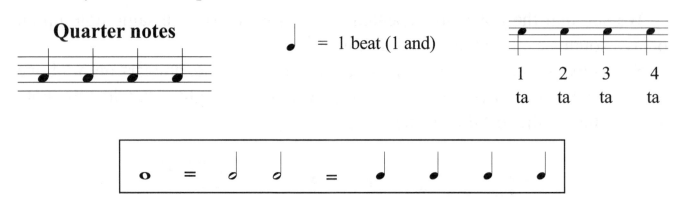

3. 4/4 Time Signature, Measure, Bar Line

The Time signature appears at the beginning of the music after the clef sign. It contains two numbers, one above the other.

The upper number tells how many beats (or counts) are in each measure. In this case, 4.

The lower number indicates what type of note receives 1 beat. In this case, a quarter note.

The two numbers in the time signature are often replaced by the letter **C**.

$$\frac{4}{4} = C$$

Music is divided into equal parts by **Bar lines.** The area between the two bar lines is called **a Measure** or **Bar.**

The End Bar line is written at the end of a piece of music. It is made up of one thin and one thick line, with the thick line always on the outside.

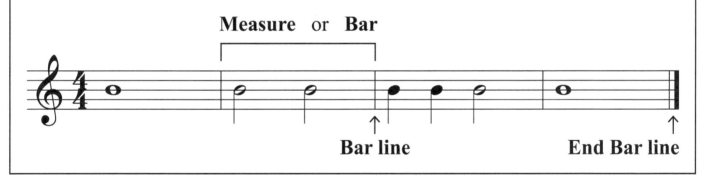

Measure or Bar

Bar line   End Bar line

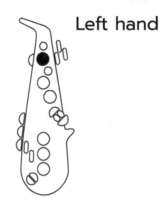

Left hand

Watch the video

Fingering chart

Practice Long Tones

It is important to practice playing **long notes.** These are notes played as long as you exhale. The long note exercise is practiced at the beginning of every saxophone lesson.

Play B ——————————— Take a breath ——————————— Etc.

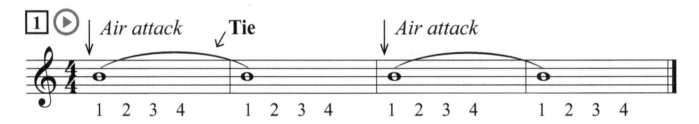

A Tie joins two notes of the same pitch by a curved line over or under the notes. Each note joined by a tie is held for its full value but only the first note is played or sung. The tied note's value is added to the value of the first note.

Metronome
100 Beats per Minute
for Exercises

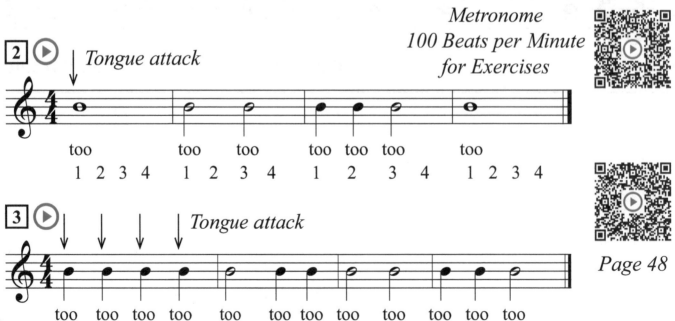

Page 48

4. Rests

Music is not only made up of sounds, but also the silence between sounds. The duration of musical silence is determined by the value of **the Rest.**

A whole rest means to rest for a whole measure. It hangs down from the 4th line.	
An half rest is equal to half of a whole rest. It sits on the 3rd line.	
A quarter rest is equal to one quarter of a whole rest.	

In 4/4 Time:

Quarter rest are equal to 1 beat.	1 2 3 4
Half rest is equal to 2 beats.	1 2 3 4
Whole rest is equal to 4 beats.	1 2 3 4

1 Quarter Note = 1 beat   1 Quarter Rest = 1 silent beat

Clap the rhythm while counting

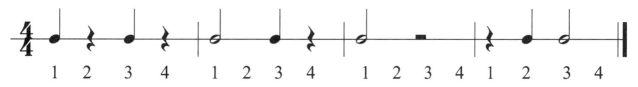

1   2   3   4   1   2   3   4   1   2   3   4   1   2   3   4

49

The Note A

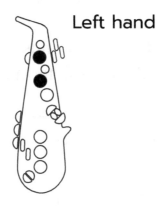

Left hand

Pages 50-53

1 ▶

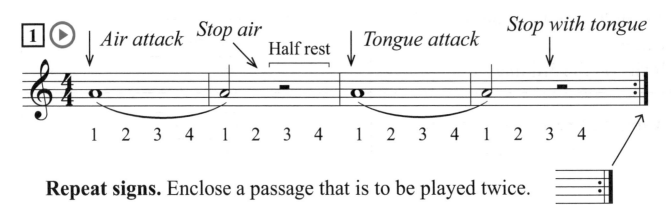

| Air attack | Stop air | Half rest | Tongue attack | Stop with tongue |

1 2 3 4 1 2 3 4 1 2 3 4 1 2 3 4

Repeat signs. Enclose a passage that is to be played twice.

Play long notes while gradually increasing volume on the first note and gradually decreasing volume on the second note.

Ending long notes is usually done without the help of the tongue, which gives a gradual fading of the sound.

Often there are indications above the notes in the form of a V or a comma, which denotes where you may take a breath.

2 ▶

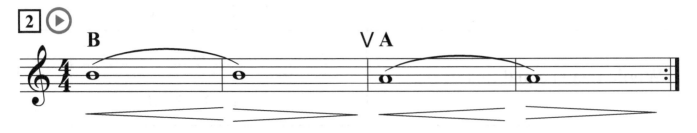

B   V A

Symbol	Italian	English
<	*crescendo*	Gradually get louder
>	*diminuendo*	Gradually get softer

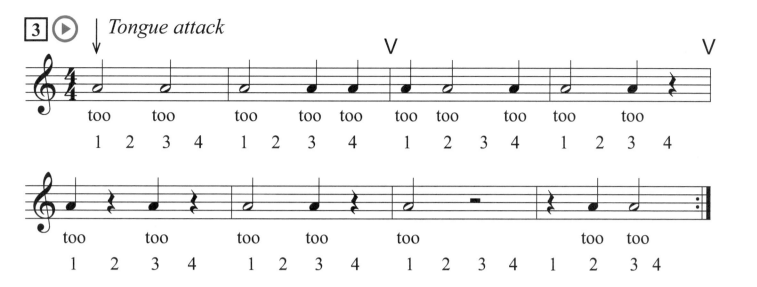

5. Eighth Note

When you add a flag to the stem of a quarter note, it becomes **an eighth note.**

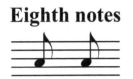

Stem → Flag ← Note head

Two Eighth notes equal the duration of one quarter note. An eighth note is equal to one-half a count (or beat).

Eighth notes

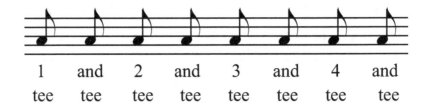

Count (1 and 2 and 3 and 4 and) and clap the rhythm evenly (once per beat and once per "and"). The beat numbers are written under the notes. Also, say "tee" and clap.

1	and	2	and	3	and	4	and
tee	tee	tee	tee	tee	tee	tee	tee

Two or more 8th notes are connected by a beam.

Beam

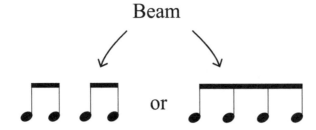

or

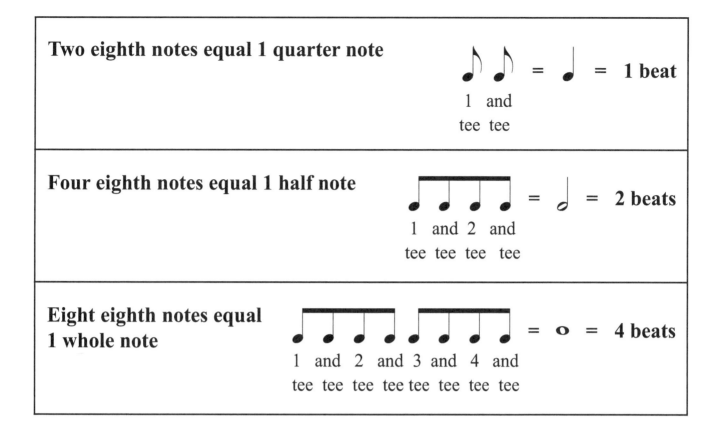

Two eighth notes equal 1 quarter note	♪ ♪ = ♩ = 1 beat
Four eighth notes equal 1 half note	♫♫ = 𝅗𝅥 = 2 beats
Eight eighth notes equal 1 whole note	♫♫♫♫ = 𝅝 = 4 beats

Two eighth notes equal 1 quarter note
1 and
tee tee

Four eighth notes equal 1 half note
1 and 2 and
tee tee tee tee

Eight eighth notes equal 1 whole note
1 and 2 and 3 and 4 and
tee tee tee tee tee tee tee tee

Clap the rhythm while counting

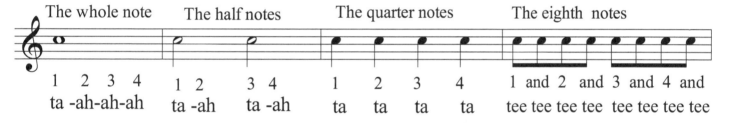

The whole note   The half notes   The quarter notes   The eighth notes
1 2 3 4   1 2   3 4   1   2   3   4   1 and 2 and 3 and 4 and
ta -ah-ah-ah   ta -ah   ta -ah   ta ta ta ta   tee tee tee tee tee tee tee tee

5 ▶

A A B A B A   B B B B A   ∨B   A A   B B B A   ∨
1 & 2 & 3 & 4 & 1 & 2 & 3 & 4 & 1 & 2 & 3 & 4 & 1 & 2 & 3 & 4 &

B B A   A B A B A   ∨B   A   B   A   A
1 & 2 & 3 & 4 & 1 & 2 & 3 & 4 & 1 & 2 & 3 & 4 & 1 & 2 & 3 & 4 &

53

The Note G

Practice long tone

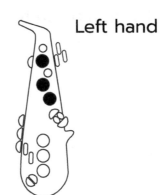

Left hand

Pages 54-55

1 ▶

G   ∨ G   ∨ A   ∨ B

2 ▶

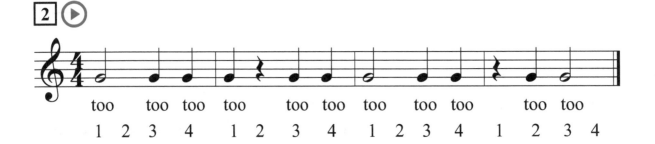

too   too   too   too   too   too   too   too   too   too   too

1   2   3   4   1   2   3   4   1   2   3   4   1   2   3   4

Clap the rhythm while counting

1 & 2 & 3 & 4 &   1 & 2 & 3 & 4 &   1 & 2 & 3   & 4 &   1 & 2 & 3 & 4 &

3 ▶

G   G   A   A A B   B   ∨ A A   A G A   A   B   A   G   ∨

1   2   3   4   1 & 2   3   4   1 & 2 & 3   4   1   2   3   4

G   A   B B B B B   A   ∨ A A A A A   G   G

1   2   3   4   1 & 2 & 3   4   1 & 2 & 3   4   1   2   3   4

54

Now you can play these songs:

Hot Cross Buns

Hot cross buns! Hot cross buns! One a pen-ny, two a pen-ny, hot cross buns!

Down By the Station

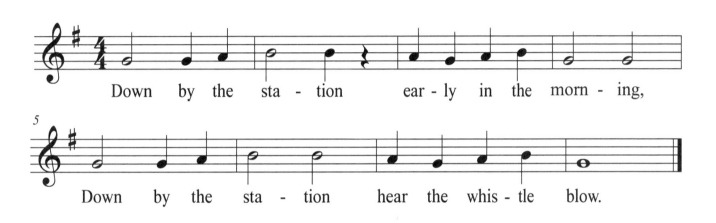

Down by the sta - tion ear - ly in the morn - ing,

Down by the sta - tion hear the whis - tle blow.

Sleep, Baby Sleep

Traditional

Sleep, ba - by sleep, The fath - er tends the sheep.

Moth - er shakes the dream-land tree, And down fall pleas - ant

dreams for thee, Sleep, ba - by, sleep.

6. ²⁄₄ and ³⁄₄ Time Signatures

²   2 means that there are 2 beats per measure;
₄   4 means that the quarter note receives 1 beat.

²⁄₄ and ⁴⁄₄ both have 4 as the bottom number, meaning a quarter note receives 1 beat. <u>The difference is that:</u> ²⁄₄ has 2 beats per measure while ⁴⁄₄ has 4.

A whole rest is used for a full measure of rest even if there are only 2 beats in each measure. When writing music, a half rest and a whole note are never used in ²⁄₄ time.

---

3   3 means that there are 3 beats per measure;
₄   4 means that the quarter note receives 1 beat.

A whole rest is used for a full measure of rest, even if there are only 3 beats in each measure. When writing the music, a half rest and a whole note are never used in ³⁄₄ time.

²⁄₄, ³⁄₄ and ⁴⁄₄ all have 4 as the bottom number, meaning the quarter note always receives 1 beat.

The Note C

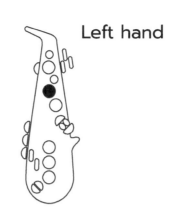

Left hand

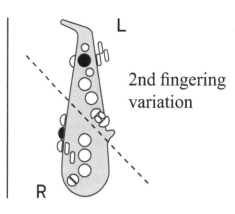

L

2nd fingering variation

R

Practice long tone

Play C

too
1 2 3 4
too
1 2 3 4
too too too
1 2 3 4
too too too
1 & 2 3 4

Barcarolle ▶

Jacques Offenbach

1 2 3   1 2 3   1 2 3   1 2 3

1 2 3   1 2 3   1 2 3   1 2 3

Waltz ▶

Avgusta Udartseva

Page 57

C G A G C   B G A G B   ∨ A C B A G A   G C G   ∨

1 & 2 & 3 &   1 & 2 & 3 &   1 & 2 & 3 &   1 & 2 & 3 &

A B C A C A   G A G   ∨ B A G A B G   C   ∨

1 & 2 & 3 &   1 & 2 & 3 &   1 & 2 & 3 &   1 & 2 & 3 &

57

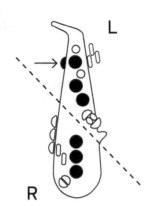

You need to add the
Octave key (left thumb)

Practice long tone

Play D

too too too too too too too too too

1 2 3 4 1 2 3 4 1 2 3 4 1 2 3 4

God Is So Good

God is so good, God is so good,

God is so good, He's so good to me.

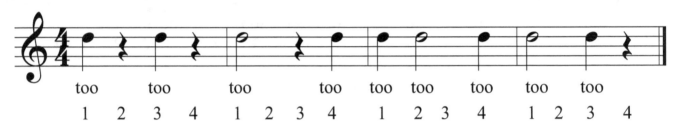

Pages 58-59

Ode to Joy ▶

Ludwig van Beethoven

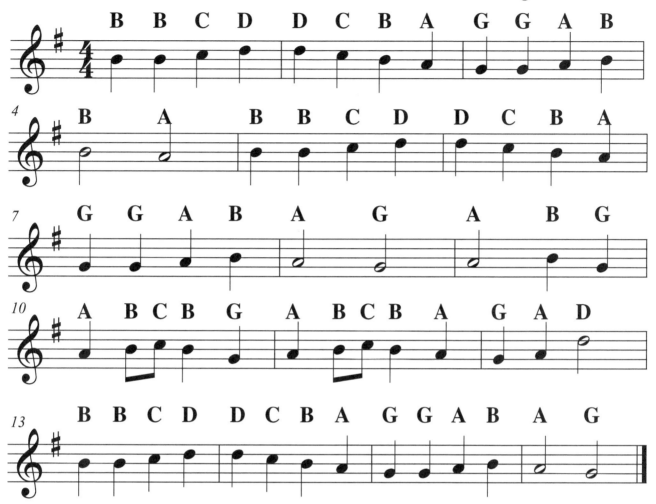

Remember

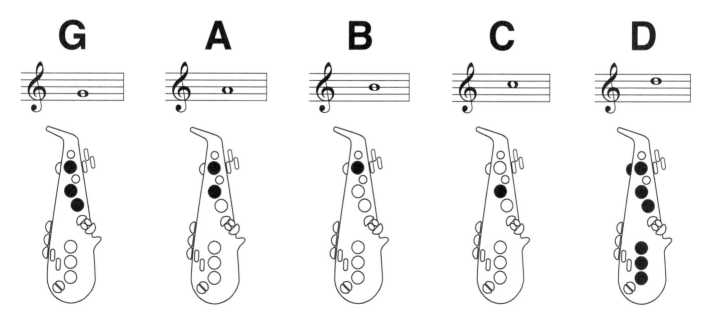

The Note F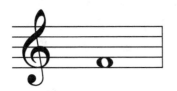

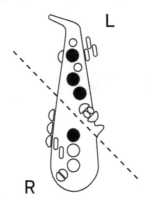

Page 60

Practice long tone

Play F

too   too too too   too   too too too too   too too   too too too

Mary Had a Little Lamb ▶

Sarah Josepha Hale
1866

A G F G A A A   G G G   A C C

Ma - ry had a lit - tle lamb,   lit - tle lamb, lit - tle lamb,

A G F G A A A A G G A G F   F

Ma - ry had a lit - tle lamb, its fleece was white as snow. And

A G F G A A A   G G G   A C C

eve - ry - where that Ma - ry went,   Ma - ry went, Ma - ry went,

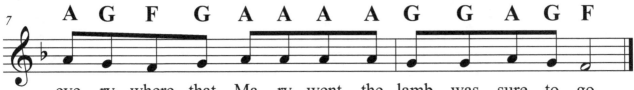

A G F G A A A A G G A G F

eve - ry - where that Ma - ry went, the lamb was sure to go.

60

How to Play Low Notes

1. Inhale through the mouth (upper teeth remain on the mouthpiece, lower jaw is open);
2. Maintain constant air pressure using your abdominal muscles;
3. When exhaling, do not clamp the reed tightly or tense the muscles of the lower jaw;
4. Avoid rapid airflow as you begin exhaling;
5. The air outflow should feel as if you were fogging a mirror rather than blowing out a candle.

The Note E

Page 61

Practice long tone

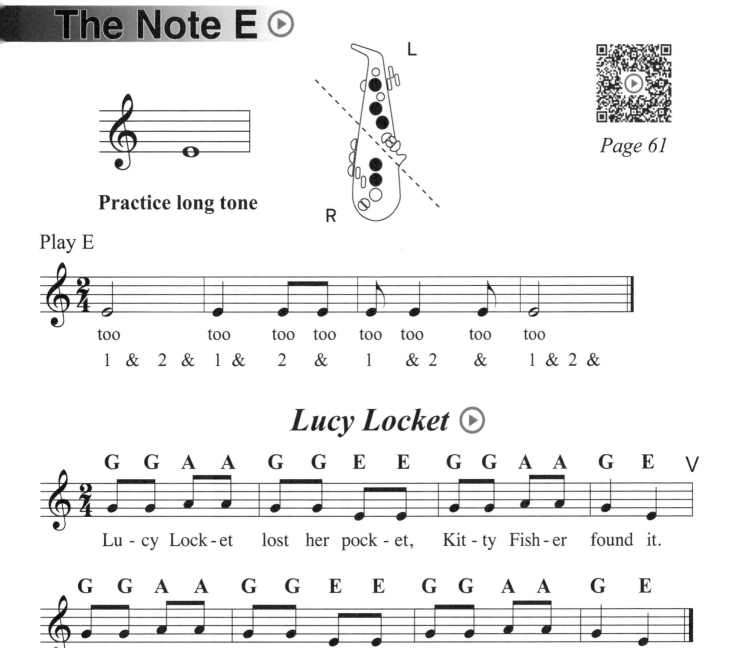

Play E

too   too   too too   too too   too   too

1 & 2 & 1 & 2 & 1 & 2 & 1 & 2 &

Lucy Locket

G G A A G G E E G G A A G E

Lu - cy Lock - et   lost her pock - et,   Kit - ty Fish - er   found it.

G G A A G G E E G G A A G E

Not a pen - ny was there in it,   on - ly rib - bon round it.

The Note D ▶

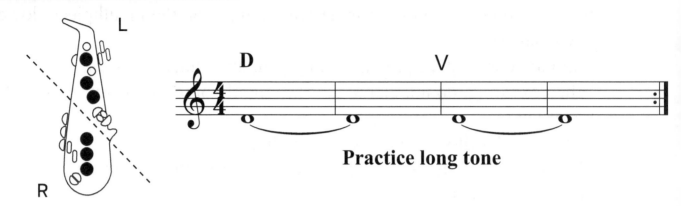

Practice long tone

Waltz (1) ▶

Avgusta Udartseva

The Note C ▶

Pages 62-63

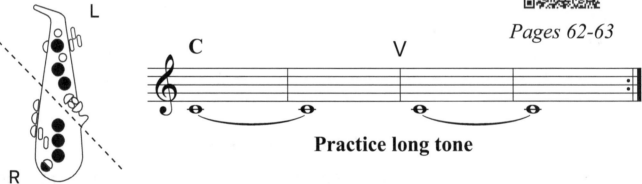

Practice long tone

Waltz (2) ▶

Avgusta Udartseva

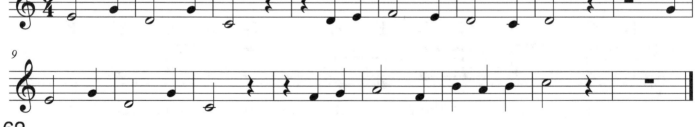

C major scale

Scale - a set of notes that are ordered by pitch.

Now you know how to play the basic notes and this sequence forms the C major scale.

Play each note at a slow tempo starting with the bottom C.

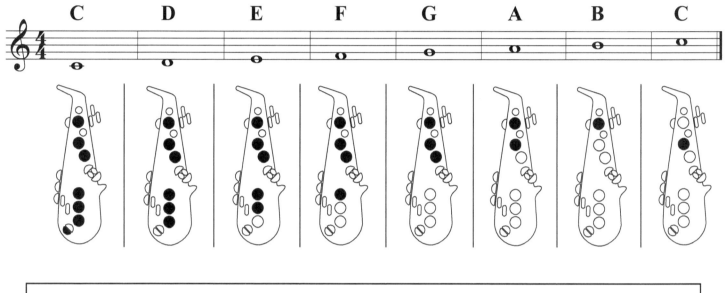

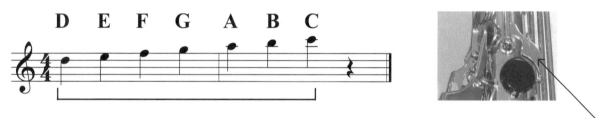

The fingering of these notes in the second octave is the same as the fingering of the same notes in the first octave, but you need to add an Octave key (left thumb).

Practice scales until you feel comfortable and familiar with the progressions and can play each note with a consistent pitch.

Play the C major scale in 2 octaves ▶

There are other major scales, but we'll talk about them in more detail in Part 2 of this book (Pages 123-124).

All of the major scales are covered on page 218.

7. Sharp, Flat and Enharmonic Notes

The Sharp sign (♯) before a note raises the pitch of that note.

The Flat sign (♭) before a note lowers the pitch of that note.

The note which is half a step higher than D is D sharp. On the piano this is the black key to the immediate right of D. The note which is half step lower than E is E flat. On the piano this is the black key to the immediate left of E.

But isn't this the same key? Why do they have different names, you might ask. There's a term used to describe this and it's called enharmonics. D sharp and E flat are enharmonic equivalents because while they are played by the same key, they have different note names.

Enharmonic notes - two notes that sound the same but are written differently.

On the Saxophone just as on the keyboard, one combination of closed holes can be written in two ways (a note with a flat or a note with a sharp). Here are the five basic pairs.

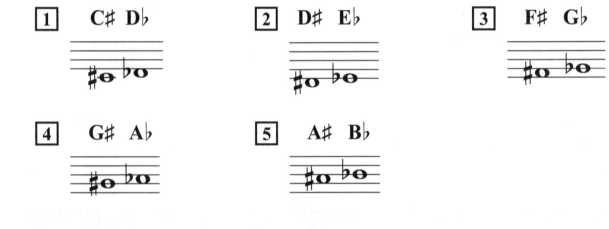

There's D-Flat (or C-Sharp), E-Flat (or D-Sharp), G-Flat (or F-Sharp), A-Flat (or G-Sharp) and B-Flat (or A-Sharp).

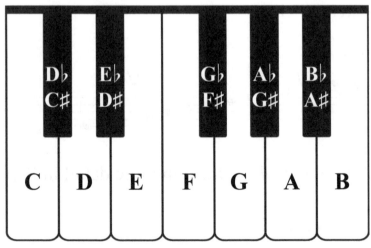

64

8. Key Signatures

Usually certain sharps or flats are used throughout the piece. Writing in those sharps or flats every time they appear takes time and adds clutter. Instead, composers put them in a key signature found just after the clef at the beginning of each stave. Key signatures tell us what notes are always sharp or flat in a given piece of music. Always read the sharps or flats in a key signature. Key signatures always have the sharps and flats listed in the same order. They always follow the same pattern.

The Sharps ♯

The Flats ♭

Natural ♮

♮ This sign overrides all previous signs (flats or sharps) in a measure.

The Note F#

Pages 66-67

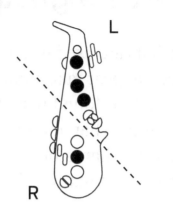

L

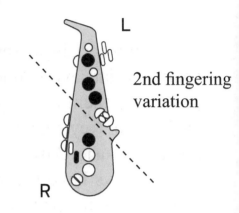

L

2nd fingering variation

Rain, Rain, Go Away ▶

A   F#   A   A   F#   A   A   F#   B   A   A   F#

Rain, rain, go a - way, come a - gain a - noth - er day.

G   G   E   E   G   G   E   A   G   F#   E   F#   D   D

Lit - tle child - ren want to play, Rain__ Rain__ go a - way.

London Bridge Is Falling Down ▶

A   B   A   G   F#   G   A   E   F#   G   F#   G   A

Lon - don Bridge is fall - ing down, fall - ing down, fall - ing down,

A   B   A   G   F#   G   A   E   A   F#   D

Lon - don Bridge is fall - ing down, My fair la - dy.

Each note joined by a tie is held for its full value but only the first note is played. The tied note's value is added to the value of the first note.

Tie

1   2   3   4   1   2   3   & 4

66

9. Articulation

Articulation - the manner in which a note is performed.

Non Legato - the sounds are pronounced separately using the tongue. The duration of the note is fully sustained.

1 ▶ Play the G major scale. All Tongued

G A B C D E F♯ G F♯ E D C B A G

A slur smoothly connects two or more notes of different pitches by a curved line over or under the notes. There is no break in sound between pitches. This is also called playing or singing **legato.** A smooth connection of sounds without using the tongue.

2 ▶ Slur ↘   All Slurred

Melody ▶

A. G. Rubinstein

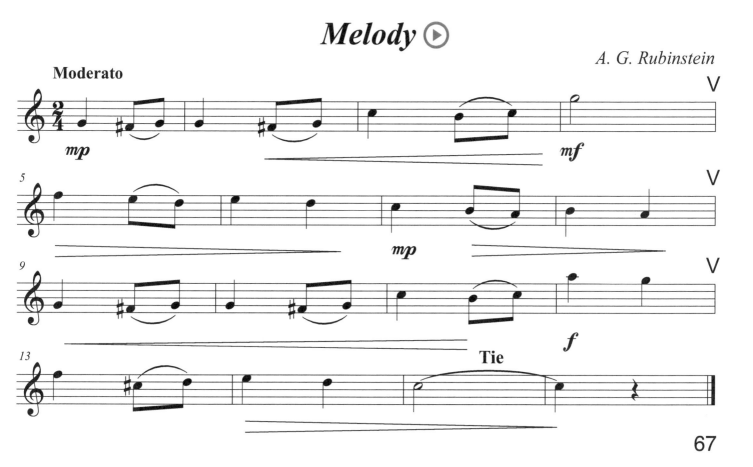

Tongue stop

Dots placed above or below note heads indicate that the notes should be played **staccato,** in a detached manner. Musicians often play a staccato quarter note as if it were an eighth note followed by an eighth rest. Short sound with a firm attack and a clear ending with the tongue, from Italian "staccato" - torn off, separated.

Golden Sun ▶

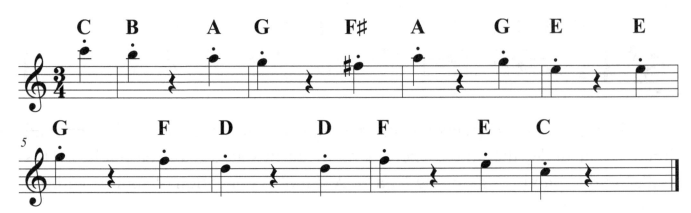

Held for full duration

Tenuto - the duration of the note is fully sustained. Sounds are extracted similarly to non legato, but more connected, gently separating each note with the tongue.

> •

Heavy Accent, play full length

Accent - accented, emphatically firm attack of sound, duration is not shortened.

∧ •

Heavy staccato accent, play short (Tongue stop)

Marcato (accented, emphasized hard attack of sound, from the Italian "marcato" - marked).

A sharper, shorter and firmer accent, played as a bright staccato.

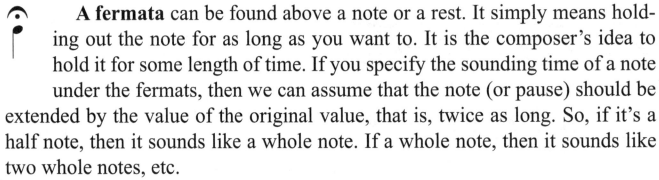

A fermata can be found above a note or a rest. It simply means holding out the note for as long as you want to. It is the composer's idea to hold it for some length of time. If you specify the sounding time of a note under the fermats, then we can assume that the note (or pause) should be extended by the value of the original value, that is, twice as long. So, if it's a half note, then it sounds like a whole note. If a whole note, then it sounds like two whole notes, etc.

Early One Morning

English folk song

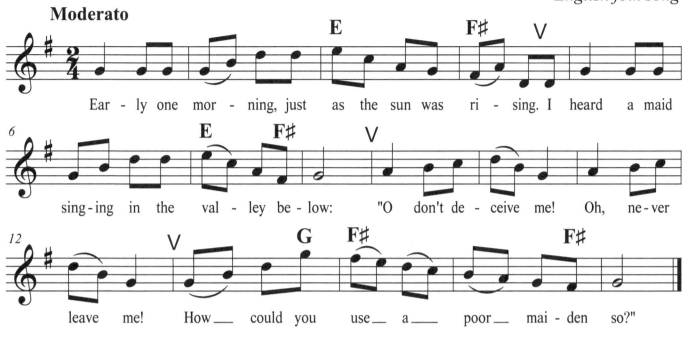

Ear - ly one mor - ning, just as the sun was ri - sing. I heard a maid

sing - ing in the val - ley be - low: "O don't de - ceive me! Oh, ne - ver

leave me! How ___ could you use ___ a ___ poor ___ mai - den so?"

Eighth Rest

An eighth rest ♪ is equal to half the value of a quarter rest 𝄽

Two 8th rests equal 1 quarter rest

Four 8th rests equal 1 half rest

Eight 8th rests equal 1 whole rest

Eighth rests   **Eighth notes**

Clap and play

Pages 68-69

69

Sixteenth Note

 Sixteenth note = 1/4 beat

1   and   2   and   3   and   4   and

♩ = ♪♪ = ♪♪♪♪

1 and   1 and   1   and

Clap the rhythm while counting

1   & 2 & 3 & 4   &   1 & 2   & 3 & 4   &   1& 2& 3   &   4&   1& 2 & 3& 4&

A sixteenth rest is equal to half the value of an eighth rest

𝄾 = 𝄾 𝄾   𝄽 = 𝄾 𝄾 = 𝄾 𝄾 𝄾 𝄾

Clap the rhythm while counting

1   & 2 & 3& 4   &   1 & 2 & 3 & 4   &   1& 2& 3 & 4&   1& 2 & 3& 4&

10. Dotted Note

A dot is placed after the note to indicate a change in the duration of a note. The dot adds half of the value of the note to itself. For example, a dotted half note gets 3 beats - the value of a half note is 2, half of 2 is 1 so 2 + 1 = 3.

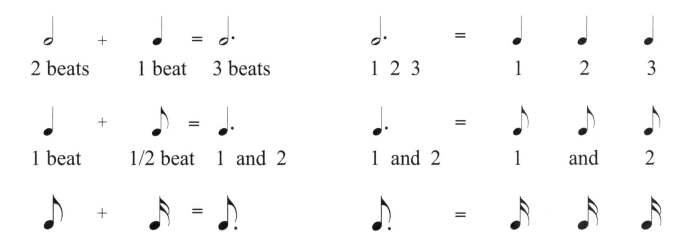

Clap the rhythm while counting

Dotted rhythms mix longer dotted notes with shorter undotted notes.

Clap the rhythm while counting

Clap the rhythm while counting

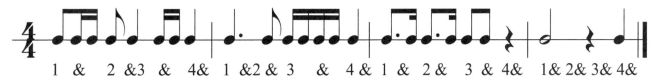

71

11. $\frac{6}{8}$ Time Signature

$\frac{6}{8}$ 6 means that there are 6 beats per measure;
8 means that the eighth note receives 1 beat.

Underline{How to count in $\frac{6}{8}$}:

There are two ways to count a bar in $\frac{6}{8}$ time. This can seem confusing when you first encounter it, but as we'll see the difference is not as big as it first appears.

You can either count it as:

• 6 eighth-note beats: 1, 2, 3, 4, 5, 6 = 1, 2, 3, 1, 2, 3
• 2 dotted-quarter-note beats: 1… 2…

Clap and say the beats

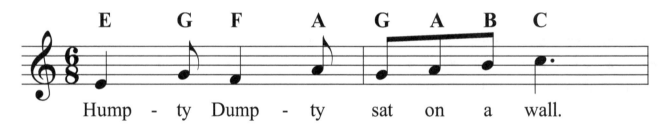

Play

Humpty Dumpty ▶

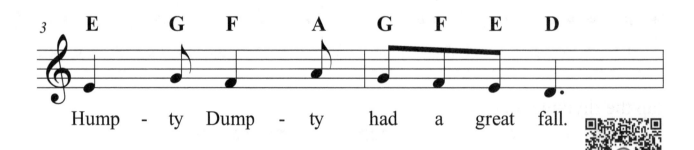

Pages 72-73

12. Numbering of Measures

In this collection, the bars in each song are numbered. At the beginning of each next line of notes, a number is placed above the treble clef, which indicates the number of the measure.

The numbering of measures in the first note line is not indicated.

Play

Aura Lee

music by George R. Poulton;
lyrics by W. W. Fosdick

13. Incomplete Measure

A Measure is a unit of music. It is the space (area of music) between two bar lines. The time signature (the 2 numbers at the beginning of the melody) indicates how many beats are in a measure.

A first measure is called **an incomplete measure** when it does not contain the full number of beats as indicated by the time signature.

The notes in the first incomplete measure (the part of the counts found at the beginning of the music) are called *the anacrusis,* pick-up or upbeat.

An incomplete measure is a measure that is split or divided between the beginning and the end of the music.

Part of the measure is found at the beginning of the music. The remaining part of the measure is found at the end of the music.

The two "parts" must add up to one complete (full) measure.

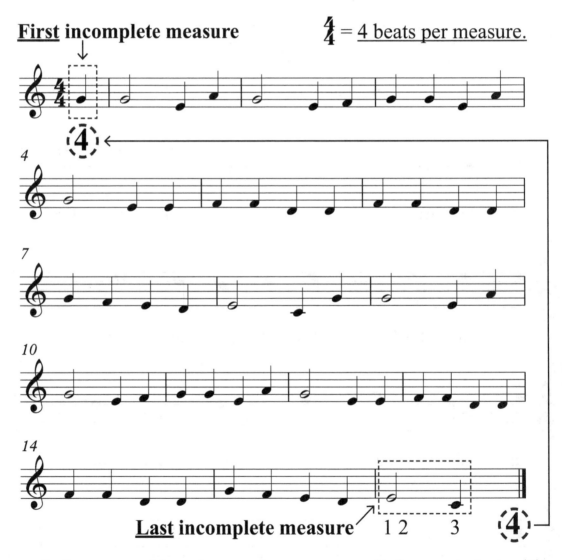

When a melody starts with an incomplete measure, it does not start with count #1!

74

Count #1 is the first count of the first complete measure. It is not necessarily the first count of the melody.

So, how is the first count of an incomplete measure? To figure this out, you must go to the end, to the last measure!

$\frac{3}{4}$ = 3 beats per measure.

Happy Birthday to You ▶

Pages 75-78

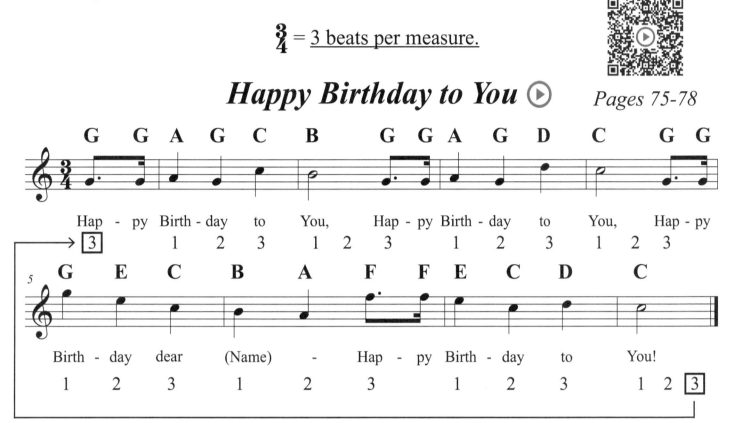

The beginning of the final measure will be count #1. So, start adding the counts there and, when you run out of beats, head back to the beginning and finish adding the counts.

The final measure will start with count #1. Start adding the counts there and, when they run out of notes to write counts under, they head back to the beginning to finish the counting.

Why do we use an incomplete measure? Quite simply, it is all about the beat and the pulse. Trying to sing "Happy Birthday" but start with a strong downbeat (strong pulse) instead of starting with a weak upbeat (weak pulse). It just does not sound correct, does it?

The important tip to remember is that measure #1 is the first measure that has count #1! The first measure may not be measure #1. If there is no count #1 at the beginning of that measure, then it is an incomplete measure.

The anacrusis, upbeat or first incomplete measure will not have a measure number. It is considered part of the final measure (the last incomplete measure) when counting measures.

So, while it looks like there are 9 measures in this melody, there are only 8 complete measures.

Happy Birthday to You

14. Triplets

Notes normally divide into two or four equal parts.

1 and 1 and 1 and

Triplets can be used to divide a note into three equal parts.

Triplets are indicated as three notes enclosed in square brackets and marked with the number 3.

Quarter note = Two eighth notes = Three eighth-note triplets

Wedding March

Felix Mendelssohn

First and Second Endings

A repeated passage is to be played with a different ending on the second time.

Play from measure 1-6, then play the first ending of measure 7-8. Since there are repeat dots, go back to the beginning and play measures 1-6, and then play the second ending, measures 9-10.

Jingle Bells ▶

Jin - gle bells,   jin - gle bells,   jin - gle all   the

way!   Oh, what fun   it   is   to ride   in a

one   horse   o - pen   sleigh! Hey!

one - horse   o - pen   sleigh!

The Note B♭

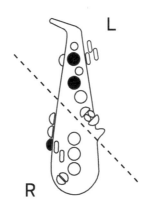

Page 79

These exercises are designed to train articulation, combining both tonguing and slurring:

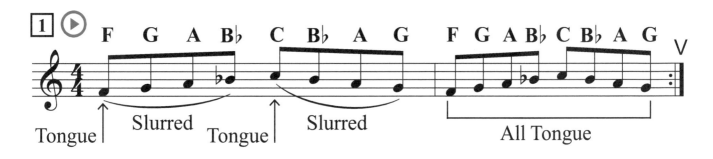

Finlandia

Jean Sibelius

80

15. *8ᵛᵃ* in Music

Sign *8ᵛᵃ* – – – is used for convenience of reading musical notation. This makes playing notes easier and faster. An *8ᵛᵃ* is a musical symbol used to tell you to play the exact same notes as written, but an octave (an octave is 8 notes) either higher or lower. The *8ᵛᵃ* sign simplifies written music for the composer. Instead of having multiple ledger lines extending higher and higher up, the music can be written much more simply with an *8ᵛᵃ*.

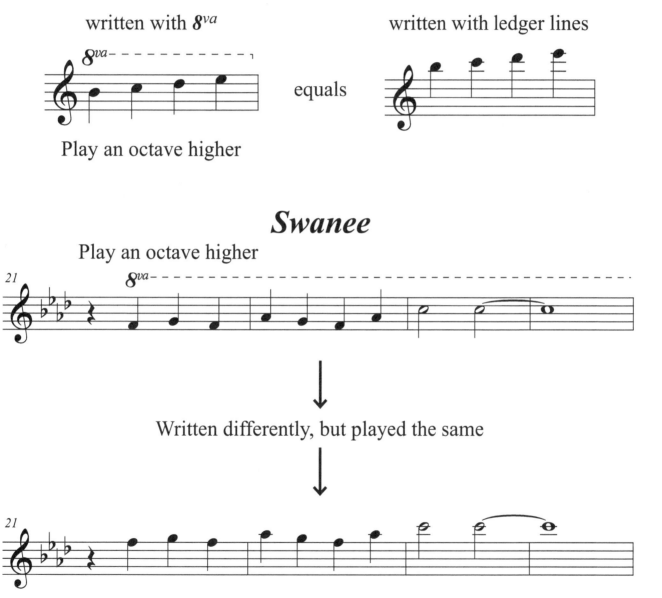

written with *8ᵛᵃ*

Play an octave higher

equals

written with ledger lines

Swanee

Play an octave higher

Written differently, but played the same

16. Tempo

Tempo is a word meaning "tempo of speed", i. e., how fast or slow to play the music.

You must learn to play a piece of music at different tempos. To truly master your instrument, you must be able to play as convincingly at high speed as at low speed, and vice versa. Usually, musicians practice playing at different tempos, and a device such as a metronome helps them do this.

A metronome is a device that produces a click at a regular interval of time. Mechanical metronomes have a pendulum that swings back and forth. You can also use an electronic metronome or even a metronome app on your phone. If you play an electronic piano, then it should have a function called "Metronome".

For example, one click is equal to one quarter note. Thus, in 4/4 meter (the most common time signature), each metronome click equals one quarter note, and four clicks equal a full bar.

If you see the designation above the notes that 1 quarter equals 60, then the metronome should make 60 beats per minute, that is, one beat is synchronic with a second. In this case, 1 beat of the metronome is a quarter note.

$$\quarternote = 60$$

You can select a different duration for 1 beat of the metronome. Sometimes it is preferred that metronome clicks represent an eighth note, a dotted quarter note, or a half note.

$$\quarternote. = 50$$

1 metronome beat is equal to ♩.
50 beats per minute

$$\halfnote. = 60$$

1 metronome beat is equal to 𝅗𝅥.
60 beats per minute

But usually they indicate a quarter note (1 beat of the metronome). It is more convenient if the tempo is not very fast. It is often set to ♩ = 90, 120, 140 beats per minute, but you can set the tempo that suits you. A metronome can help you keep a consistent tempo so that you won't inadvertently speed up or slow down.

Italian Tempo Markings

Italian	English	Beats Per Minute
Presto	Very fast	168-208
Allegro	Fast	120-168
Moderato	Moderate speed	108-120
Andante	Moderate walking speed	76-108
Adagio	Slow (at ease)	66-76
Largo	Slow and solemn	40-66

17. Dynamics

Dynamics in music are how loud or how soft a piece of music is.

Since the first musicians that started to attempt writing music were Italian, the terms are still used today. So now when you look at music, you will discover a lot of Italian terms and writing.

List of Dynamics

Symbol	Italian	English
ppp	*pianississimo*	Very, very soft
pp	*pianissimo*	Very soft
p	*piano*	Soft
mp	*mezzo piano*	Moderately soft
mf	*mezzo forte*	Moderately loud
f	*forte*	Loud
ff	*fortissimo*	Very loud
fff	*fortississimo*	Very, very loud
<	*crescendo*	Gradually get louder
>	*diminuendo*	Gradually get softer
♩ >	*accent*	Play much louder
sfz	*sforzando*	Put extra emphasis on a note

On the Character of the Tone

The saxophone has a very fascinating tone, which can be both soft and clear, and sharp and edgy. Depending on the musical genre the tone of the instrument will change as well. For instance, for classical music you need a smoother, warmer, not as edgy tone. For the performance of jazz music you need a sound of a cooler shade with some edginess in it. Here an important role in the character of the tone of the saxophone is played by the mouthpiece. Each saxophone player will choose it individually, depending on his or her goals. Naturally, the manner of performance is also very important, including articulation and the sound production, since there are many ways of playing the same note (soft, sharp attack or added grace notes).

A huge role in the formation of the tone of the saxophonist plays his idea of what the instrument should sound like. To help you develop this idea you need to listen to famous performers and choose a way of playing that fits your taste, creating your own style, just as everyone has some peculiarity and his unique stroke. Keep searching for your own sound, the one that will distinguish you from other performers. The saddest thing is to play with a hollow, bored tone of voice. This is much like a painter using only with gray palette or a singer always singing with a sad, indifferent tone of voice. Often the sound of the saxophone is equated with the human voice because of its intonation features and the presence of singing vibrato. Intonation in speech and intonation in music is a very important expressive tool that helps the author or player to convey to the listener the main meaning of the work.

Why is it Good to Sing?

Sing your favorite songs whenever possible. Sing using different syllables (tah, too, tee, bee, etc.) whatever you play on the saxophone if the melody doesn't have lyrics to it. That's why there are so many songs with lyrics in this book, so that the melody is singable and you can feel the logical structure of musical phrases. The sound of the saxophone is often compared to the human voice, so the more you sing, the more natural and free the instrument will subsequently sound. The instrument is an extension of your voice, with your breath and tongue taking the lead, and the mouthpiece and reed replacing your vocal cords.

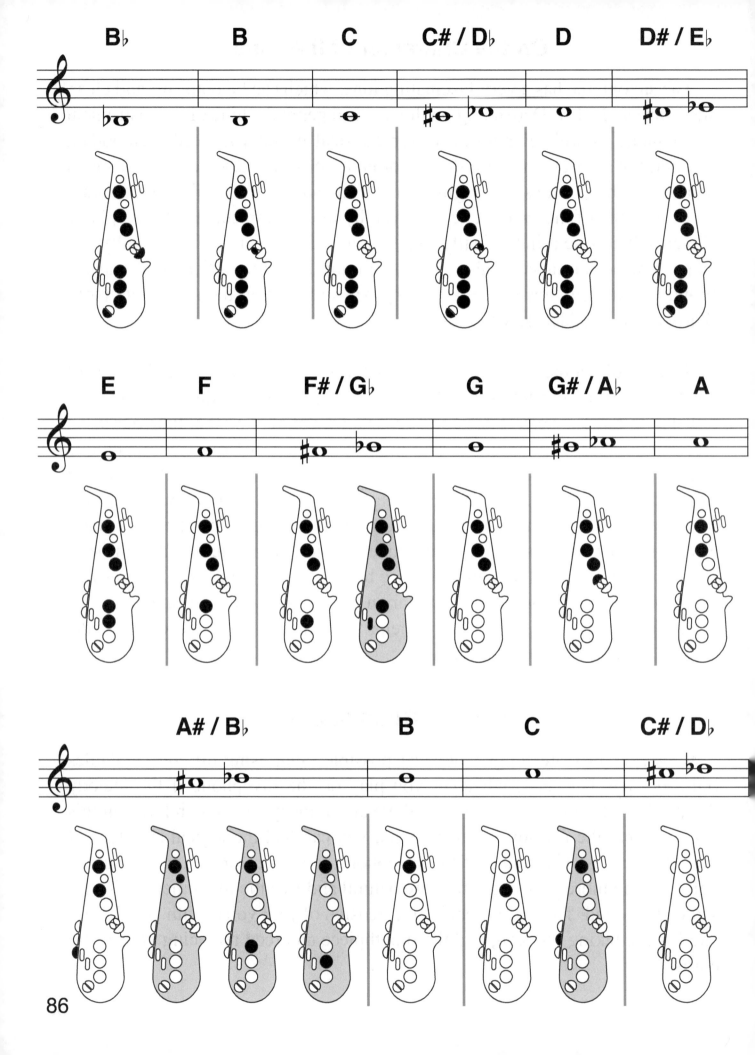

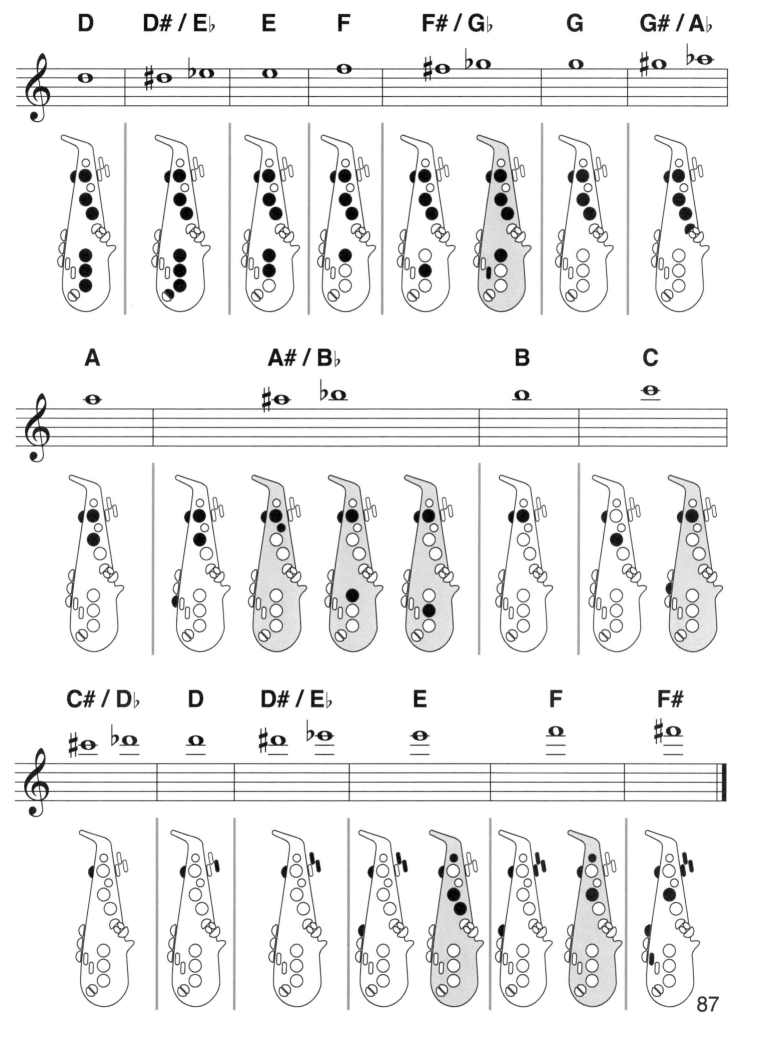

You can download the PDF *(Fingering Chart)* via a direct link:
cutt.ly/yeoGV83V
or scan the QR code:

and

Watch the video

Fingering chart

Chapter 3
Part 1 ▶

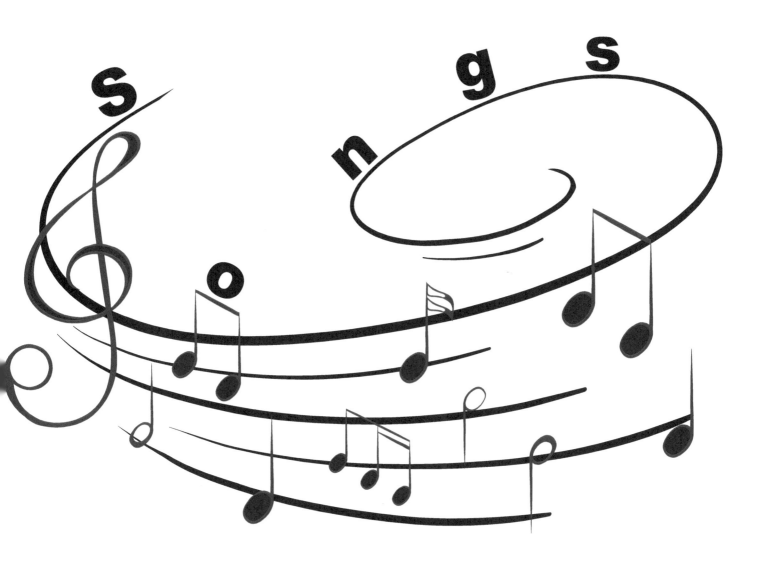

Pages 91-115
Chapter 3 - Part 1

For any questions, comments or suggestions, email us at:
avgustaudartseva@gmail.com

Scarborough Fair

Traditional

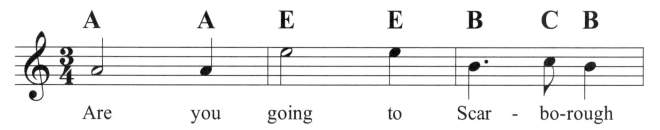

Are   you   going   to   Scar - bo-rough

Fair?   Pars - ley,   sage,   rose -

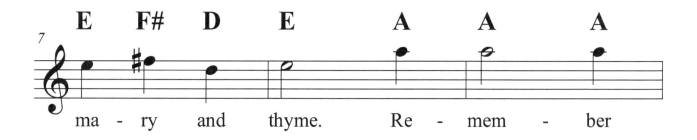

ma - ry   and   thyme.   Re - mem - ber

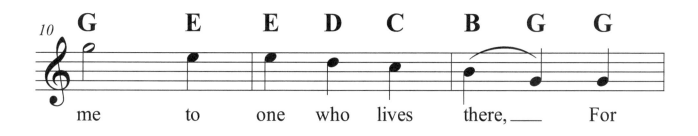

me   to   one   who   lives   there, ___   For

once   she   was   a   true   love   of   mine.

Red River Valley

Traditional

Believe Me, If All Those Endearing Young Charms

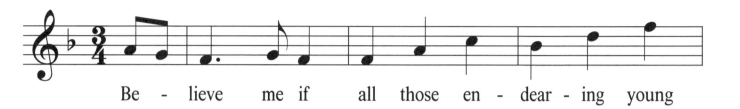

Be - lieve me if all those en - dear - ing young

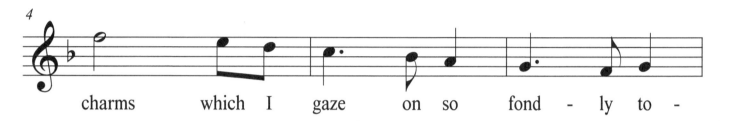

charms which I gaze on so fond - ly to -

day _____ were to change by to - mor - row and

fleet in my arms like __ fair - y gifts

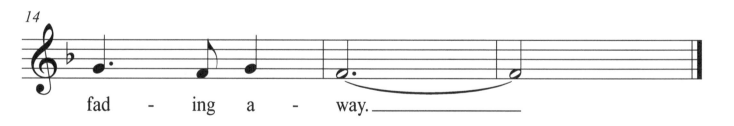

fad - ing a - way. _____

Beautiful Dreamer

Stephen C. Foster

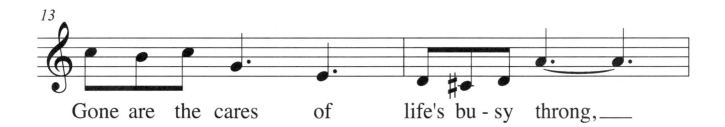

Gone are the cares of life's bu-sy throng,___

Beau-ti-ful dream-er, a-wake un-to me!___

Beau-ti-ful dream-er, a-wake un-to me!___

 *Page 94*

Sweet Betsy from Pike

American Ballad

Moderato

Oh, don't you re - mem - ber Sweet Bet - sy from Pike, who

crossed the big moun-tains with her lov - er Ike? With two yoke of

cat - tle a large yel - low dog, A tall Shang - hai roos - ter, and

one spot - ted hog. Say - ing good - bye, Pike Coun - ty fare - well for a

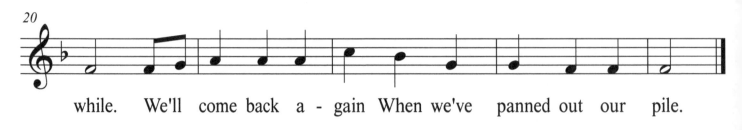

while. We'll come back a - gain When we've panned out our pile.

Page 96

Danny Boy

Traditional Irish
lyrics by Fred E. Weatherly

Greensleeves

(What Child Is This?)

Folk Song

A - las, my love,___ you do me wrong___ To

cast me off___ dis - cour - te-ous - ly For have

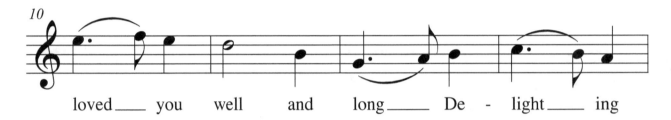

loved___ you well and long___ De - light___ ing

in___ your com - pa - ny Green sleeves was

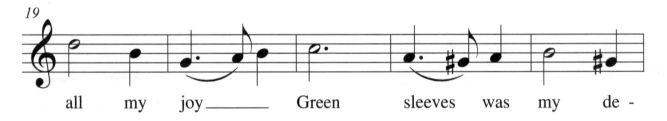

all my joy___ Green sleeves was my de -

light Green sleeves was my heart of gold___ And

who but my la___ dy green sleeves.

O Canada

music by Calixa Lavallee
lyrics by Robert Stanley Weir

Maestoso

O Can - a - da! Our home and na - tive land!

True pa - triot love in all thy sons com - mand. With

glow-ing hearts we see thee rise, the True North strong and free! From

far and wide, O___ Can - a-da, we stand on guard for thee.

God keep our land glo - rious and free!

O Can - a - da, we stand on guard for thee.

O Can - a - da, we stand on guard for thee.

Scotland the Brave ▶

Traditional Scottish

The Yellow Rose of Texas

W. Gould, 1858

There's a yel-low rose in Tex-as that I'm a-goin' to see, No oth-er dark-key-knows her, no-dark-key on-ly me. She cried so when I left her, it like to broke my heart, And if I ev-er find her we ne-ver more will part. She's the sweet-est rose of co-lor this dark-ey ev-er knew. Here eyes are bright as dia-monds, They spark-le like the dew. You talk a-bout your Di-nah And sing of Ro-sa-lie, The Yel-low Rose of Tex-as is the on-ly girl for me.

Shall We Gather at the River?

Hymn

Robert Lowry, 1964

Shall we gath-er at the riv - er, where bright an-gel feet have

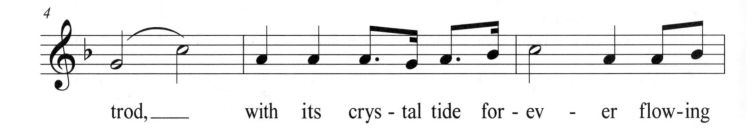

trod,___ with its crys - tal tide for - ev - er flow-ing

Refrain

by the throne of God? Yes, we'll gath-er at the riv - er, the

beau-ti-ful, the beau-ti-ful riv - er; gath-er with the saints at the

riv - er that flows by the throne of__ God.

Bring a Torch, Jeanette, Isabella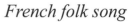

French folk song

Bring a torch,___ Jean - nette, Is - a - bel - la,

Bring a torch, to the cra - dle run!

It is Je - sus, good folk of the vil - lage,

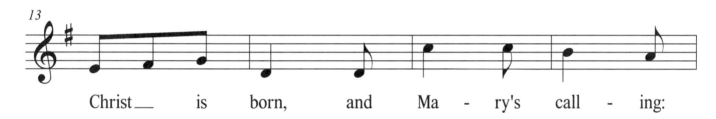

Christ___ is born, and Ma - ry's call - ing:

Ah! Ah! Beau - ti - ful is the

moth - er, Ah! Ah! Beau - ti - ful

is her Son!

The Sweet By-and-By

music by Joseph P. Webster
lyrics by S. Fillmore Bennett

Lullaby

W. A. Mozart

Marmotte ▶

L. van Beethoven

May Song

W. A. Mozart

La Paloma (The Dove) ▶

Sebastián Yradier

Page 108

Gymnopédie No. 1

Erik Satie

The Second Waltz

D. Shostakovich
arr. by Avgusta Udartseva

Sleeping Beauty Waltz

Pyotr Ilyich Tchaikovsky

Für Elise

L. van Beethoven

Chapter 2
Part 2

Theory
and
Practice

For any questions, comments or suggestions, email us at:
avgustaudartseva@gmail.com

Introduction to Part 2

In this chapter you will learn about musical intervals, the different harmonies and scales, and what pentatonics and blues pentatonics are. These topics are important for understanding the structure of melodies, the character of music, and the origin of blues tunes. You will be able to understand what a melody is made up of and what its character and mood depends on in terms of basic music theory.

If you find it too difficult or are reluctant to take up music theory at this time, you can skip the theory part and start practicing right away. You can always return to the theory later, when you feel that it is the right time and it is worthwhile to understand how the sounds are put together and work together according to certain principles.

The knowledge of music theory will give you the opportunity to understand the nature of blues intonations. You may also find it helpful should you want to start composing your own melodies and unlock the door into the world of improvisation.

1. Intervals

An interval is the distance between two notes.

The intervals are an important part of the musical vocabulary and are useful in analyzing the qualities, structure, and functions of scales, chords, and melodies.

Intervals are named by the number of the top note (2nd, 3rd, etc.) Also, the interval between identical notes is called **unison** (also called prime interval); the interval between the 1st and the 8th note is called **an octave.**

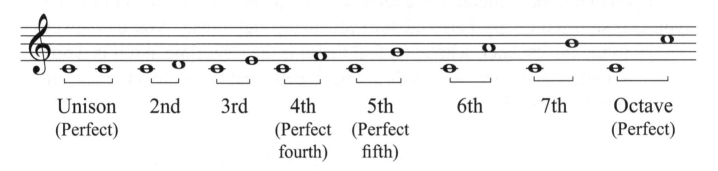

| Unison (Perfect) | 2nd | 3rd | 4th (Perfect fourth) | 5th (Perfect fifth) | 6th | 7th | Octave (Perfect) |

Intervals are measured in tones and semitones, usually counting from the lowest note to the highest.

The shortest distance between notes is half a tone (or half step). Two half tones form one full tone (or whole step).

2 Half step = 1 Whole step

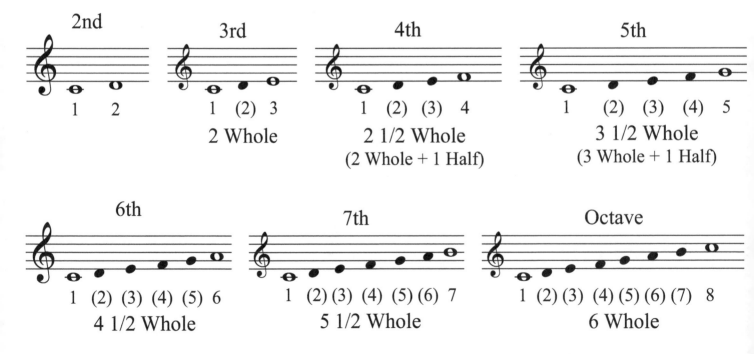

120

Intervals can be melodic (notes written in sequence, played separately) and harmonic (one note written over the other, played together).

Melodic   Harmonic

The interval between the base (first) note of a major scale and the 2nd, 3rd, 6th, or 7th note of that scale is called **a major interval.**

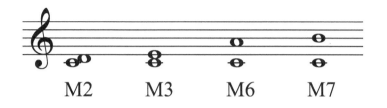

M2   M3   M6   M7

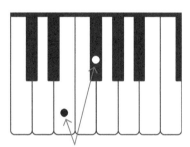

Whole Step = 2 Half Step = M2

Intervals of the major scale

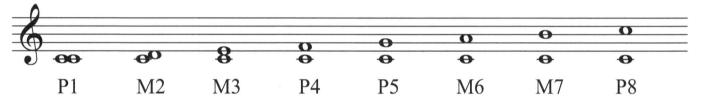

P1   M2   M3   P4   P5   M6   M7   P8

Interval Chart

Interval	Half Step	Example	Interval	Half Step	Example
Perfect prime	0	C-C	Diminished 5th (Tritone)	6	C-G♭
Minor 2nd	1	C-D♭	Perfect 5th	7	C-G
Major 2nd	2	C-D	Minor 6th	8	C-A♭
Minor 3rd	3	C-E♭	Major 6th	9	C-A
Major 3rd	4	C-E	Minor 7th	10	C-B♭
Perfect 4th	5	C-F	Major 7th	11	C-B
Augmented 4th (Tritone)	6	C-F♯	Perfect octave	12	C-C'

When a major interval (2nd, 3rd, 6th, or 7th) is reduced by half a tone, it becomes a minor interval, which is denoted by the small letter "m".

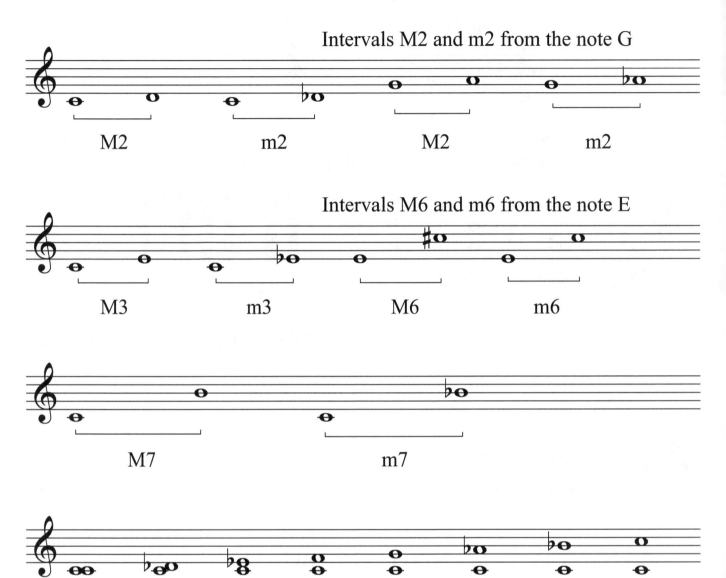

Intervals M2 and m2 from the note G

M2   m2   M2   m2

Intervals M6 and m6 from the note E

M3   m3   M6   m6

M7   m7

P1   m2   m3   P4   P5   m6   m7   P8

2. Scales and Diatonic Modes

In traditional classical music, the 7-note major sequence is called the major scale (the character of the sequence is cheerful). It is built according to the following pattern:
A whole step + whole step + half a tone + whole step + whole step + whole step + half a tone: C D E F G A B

C Major

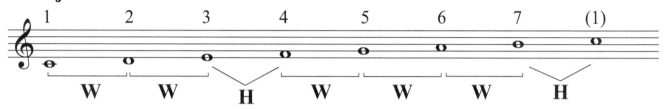

The minor scale (the character of the sound sequence is sad) is built according to the pattern:
Whole step + Half tone + Whole step + Whole step + Half tone + Whole step + Whole step + Whole step: A B C D E F G

A Minor

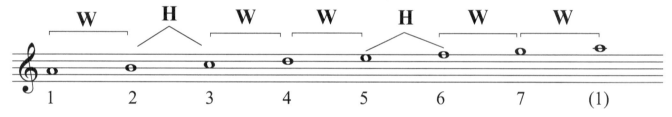

To get an idea how certain key symbols are used, we need to understand that the composer first chooses a major or minor key for his piece. Then the sharp and flat symbols logically follow from this initial choice. For example, the major key goes W, W, H, W, W, W, H. The minor key has a different structure: W, H, W, W, H, W, W.

Based on this pattern, you can build a scale from any key. There are no sharps or flats in C major and A minor. This is why these are the easiest keys to play in. However, sometimes the composer will use other keys where you can find anywhere from one to three or even four sharps or flats in the key signature.

You should learn the order of sharps in key signature notation: F♯, C♯, G♯, D♯, A♯, E♯, B♯.

The order of flats in key signature notation is the opposite of sharps: B♭, E♭, A♭, D♭, G♭, C♭, F♭.

Over time, the players memorize the key signatures of all the keys.

For example, in the D major the main note is D. There are two sharps in the key of D major: F♯ and C♯. You could always figure out the number of sharps or flats in a given key using the above pattern, i. e., building step-by-step (W,H) each note, raising (sharp) or lowering (flat) the pitch if necessary.

On the page 218 you can find all <u>the major scales</u> for reference. After C major, the next seven scales contain flats, i.e., F major has one flat, B flat major has 2 flats, and so on. The seven scales after that contain sharps, i.e., G major has one sharp, D major has two sharps, and so on.

Diatonic Modes

This topic is easiest to understand if explained using piano keys. There are a total of 7 diatonic modes, from each white key on the piano. (C D E F G A B).

A scale is the sound sequence that forms a particular mode. For example the F major scale is the Ionian mode from the F note, or D minor is the Aeolian mode but from the D note. From each note you can build one of the seven harmonies listed below. To make it easy to remember how they are formed, you need to memorize their arrangement on the white piano keys. The difference is that they will each have their own key signs. It's good to remember that C major and A minor have no additional signs, meaning that there are no sharps or flats in their respective scales.

C major (Ionian mode): the mood is cheerful.
A minor (Aeolian mode): the mood is sad.
These are the most basic modes in music, but there are other modes as well:
1. **Ionian mode** – "the major scale". All the white keys from C to C form the Ionian mode – Sounds happy.
2. **Dorian mode** – All the white keys from D to D form the Dorian mode – Sounds sad but hopeful.

3. **Phrygian mode** – All the white keys from E to E form the Phrygian mode which sounds dark.
4. **Lydian mode** – All the white keys from F to F form the Lydian mode – sounds inspiring but quirky and foreign.
5. **Mixolydian mode** – All the white keys from G to G form Mixolydian mode, which sounds happy but serious.
6. **Aeolian mode** – "the minor scale". All the white keys from A to A form the Aeolian mode, which sounds sad.
7. **Locrian mode** – All the white keys from B to B form the Locrian scale, which sounds evil and is a favorite of metal bands.

Watch the video

Modes

Mode Structure Diagram

If you memorize the order of intervals in a mode, you can play any mode, for example from the note of F or from the note of C.

Play all the harmonies from the C note and feel the mood of each mode:

Ionian – the major scale

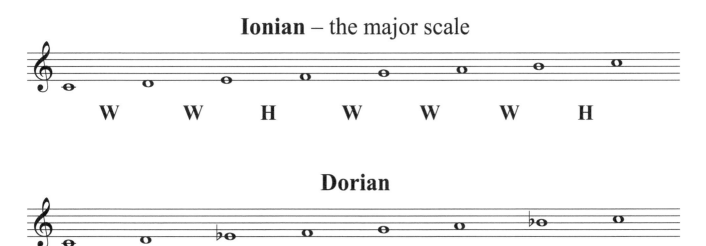

Dorian

Phrygian

H   W   W   W   H   W   W

Lydian

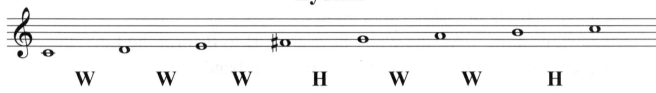

W   W   W   H   W   W   H

Mixolydian

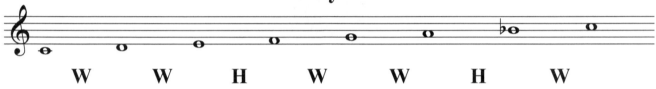

W   W   H   W   W   H   W

Aeolian – the minor scale

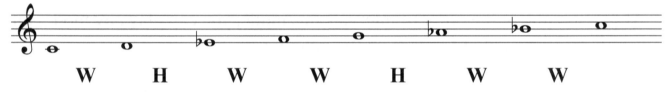

W   H   W   W   H   W   W

Locrian

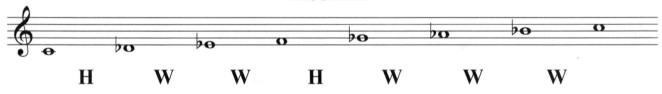

H   W   W   H   W   W   W

3. Triads and Chords

A triad is a combination of three sounds that are played together.

The saxophone is a monophonic instrument, so you can't play a triad. But you should be able to play the notes in a harmonic sequence from bottom to top, which will help you improve your technical skills and make it easier to improvise in a given harmonic sequence. For example, in a musical group all of the musicians keep the general rhythm while creating a harmonic background. At the same time the saxophone is playing solo improvisation, relying on a given harmonic sequence in the form of chords or letters denoting chords or triads.

Thus, a triad consists of a major tone (the note after which the chord is named), its 3rd (the note three steps away from the major tone), and a fifth (the note five steps away from the major tone). 1 3 5 = triad.

The root is the note from which the triad gets its name.

To build a triad, measure the 3rd and 5th upward from the root.

If the main tone is on the staff line, all the other notes of the triad will be on the line, and if the main tone is between the lines, all the other notes of the triad will be between the lines.

Root E   Root D

Triads may be built on any note of the scale.

Each letter indicates the base note from which the triad is built upward.

C major scale triads are formed from the major notes:

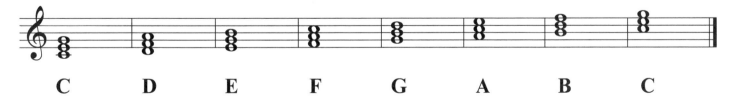

C   D   E   F   G   A   B   C

A chord is a combination of three or more sounds that sound together.

A seventh cord is a chord consisting of a triad plus a note forming an interval of a seventh above the chord's root.

The seventh chord is a chord, not a triad, because it has 4 notes, not 3.

To build a C7 chord, add a minor 7th above the root of the C triad (or a minor 3rd above the 5th).

Tonic, Subdominant and Dominant

The most important triads of any key signature are built on the 1st, 4th and 5th scale degrees of the major scale.

The three most important scale degree names are the Tonic (I), Subdominant (IV) and Dominant (V).

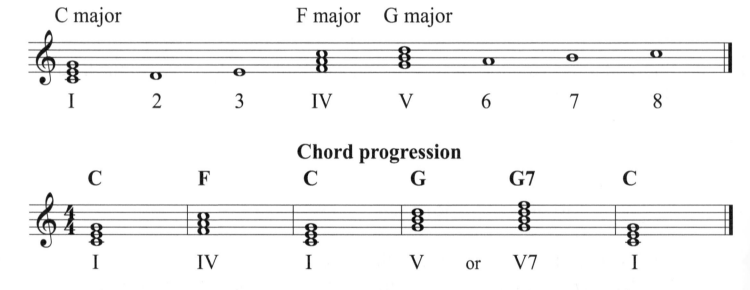

So, now you know how triads are built from any note of the scale and you know what basic chords are used to harmonize (create accompaniment for) simple melodies. Each letter represents the first root note of a chord that is in tune with the current melody in a measure. Then the chord can change in the next measure.

These designations are often added in songs and are used for guitar playing. For saxophone playing, it is a clue within which chord you can improvise or compose your own melody. Don't forget though that saxophones have their own pitch.

If the piano plays in C major, then for the Alto saxophone all the notes should be moved a major 3rd down to A major, then the pitches will match.

In this book there are often letters above the note for those who do not yet know which line the notes are on. This can serve as a hint for playing the melodies.

Inversion of Triads

The notes of each triad can be played in a different sequence, namely by moving the lower sound an octave higher to form an inversion of the triad or chord.

Triad C major

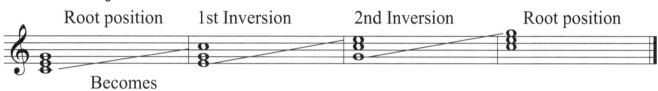

Root position: root at the bottom.
1st Inversion: 3rd down.
2nd Inversion: 5th down.

Let's play all the notes of the C major triad in order from bottom to top with its inversions.

Triad C major

C   E   G   E   G   C   G   C   E   C   E   G

Now let's play all the inversions of this triad from the 4th step (Subdominant (IV)):

Triad F major (IV)

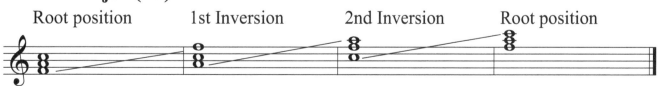

Triad F major

F   A   C   A   C   F   C   F   A   F   A   C

Now you can play the triads with inversion from the 5th step of Dominant (V):

Triad G major (V)

Root position   1st Inversion   2nd Inversion

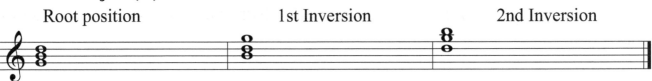

4. Arpeggios

Any successive playing of the notes of a chord can be called **an Arpeggio.**
We have already played triad conversions, now we will play arpeggios in the
same way. It is recommended that you learn arpeggios by starting to play them
three at a time (Exercise 1 below) and then four at a time (Exercises 2, 3).

C major arpeggio

131

D major arpeggio

F major arpeggio

E major arpeggio

You can also play arpeggios from each of the seventh chord's notes

C7

Be sure to play arpeggios before every lesson. This will greatly improve your technical skills. A little later you will be able to easily compose your own melodies with harmonic accompaniment.

5. Pentatonic and Blues Scales

In modern music, the pentatonic is probably the most popular mode. With the emergence of blues and jazz, and later rock and roll, rock, etc., pentatonic became one of the main modes. In this chapter you will learn about the provenance of the pentatonic and what it is.

In ancient times, the scale consisted only of a 5-note chord. Possibly, it was more convenient for composing melodies.

The pentatonic (from Greek "pente" - "five", "tonos" - "tone" - a five-step mode (a scale consisting of five steps within one octave).

The simplest explanation of the structure of the pentatonic scale would be on the piano keyboard!

If you have noticed, there are 5 black keys on the piano and they are repeated in the same sequence. If you play only the black keys from bottom to top, you will get the pentatonic - a scale of 5 sounds! If you look closely, the 5 black keys alternate with two black keys and then three black keys again and so on. If you play sequentially **Three Black Keys and then Two Black Keys,** from left to right, you will get Major Pentatonic!

The interval pattern between the notes in Major Pentatonic is as follows:

A whole step + a whole step+ three half tones (1 1/2 tones) + a whole step + 1 1/2 tones.

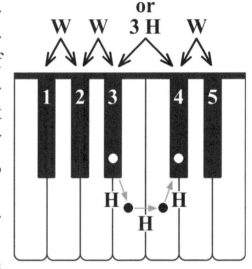

1½ Whole step = Whole + Half = 3 Half = m3

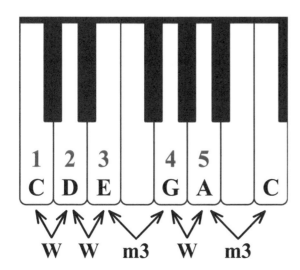

Let's transfer this diagram from the black keys to the white keys and construct a pentatonic from the note of C.

C major pentatonic

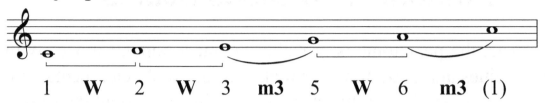

I'm suggesting a second option for understanding the structure of the major pentatonic! This is done by removing the fourth and seventh steps (notes) from the natural major scale. If you remove the notes F (4th degree) and B (7th degree) from the C major scale (C-D-E-F-G-A-B), you will get a C major pentatonic (C-D-E-G-A). (It can be derived by taking the major scale and removing the 4th and 7th degrees).

This is a five-note scale widely used in rock, blues, and jazz styles.

Minor Pentatonic

Pentatonics can be either major or minor. The minor pentatonic differs from the natural minor scale in that it lacks the second and sixth degrees.

A minor pentatonic

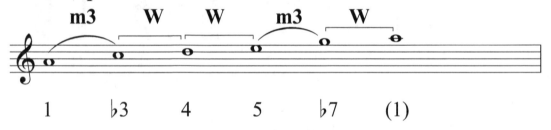

Note that from bottom to the top this scale now contains the following intervals: minor 3rd, whole step, whole step, minor 3rd, and whole step.

Parallel Scales, Pentatonics

Note that the notes in C major and A minor pentatonics are the same, the only difference is the "point of reference" - these are parallel scales. In minor pentatonic the notes are the same as in a major pentatonic, only the first step in minor pentatonic is a minor 3rd, so the character of pentatonic is already sad, minor.

m3 (minor 3rd) – The interval between major (C major) and minor pentatonics (A minor), i.e., minor pentatonic is always lower by a m3, despite the same notes and key signs. The difference is in the root note (in the example above it is the C and the A), which determines the name of the scale or the pentatonic.

By analogy, this relationship remains between other parallel scales. You could play a major pentatonic from any note (for example, from the F) and the minor pentatonic will always be a m3 lower from the first note of the major pentatonic (from F down 3 half steps is the D, so the D minor pentatonic is parallel to F major pentatonic).

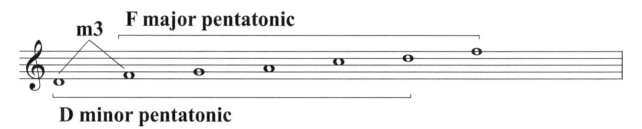

Blues Pentatonics

Pentatonics were the basis for new sound sequences – the blues major pentatonic and blues minor pentatonic!

If you lower the 3rd degree in any major pentatonic, you will get what's called a blues major pentatonic:

C blues major pentatonic

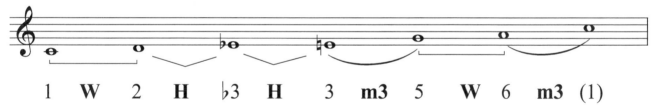

D blues major pentatonic

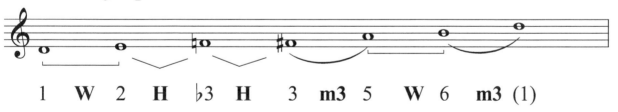

Conversely, if you raise the 4th degree (or lower the 5th degree) in a minor pentatonic, you will get a blues minor pentatonic.

Try and play a blues A minor pentatonic:

A blues

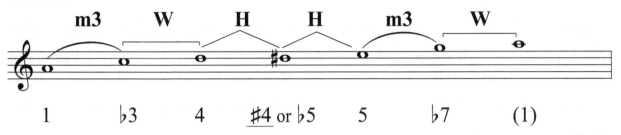

| | 1 | ♭3 | 4 | ♯4 or ♭5 | 5 | ♭7 | (1) |

Following the same pattern (with the raised 4th degree), we can build a blues minor pentatonic from the D note:

D blues minor pentatonic

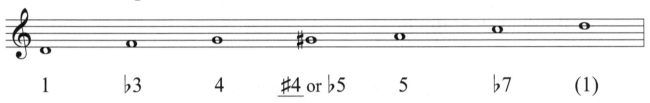

| | 1 | ♭3 | 4 | ♯4 or ♭5 | 5 | ♭7 | (1) |

For this D minor pentatonic, **a parallel Major pentatonic** will be built from the F note, which has the same notes as the D minor pentatonic, but the first note will be the note F.

F blues major pentatonic

D blues minor pentatonic

The minor pentatonic is most often used in blues tunes.

Practice playing Minor Pentatonics and Blues Minor Pentatonics from different notes:

Minor pentatonic

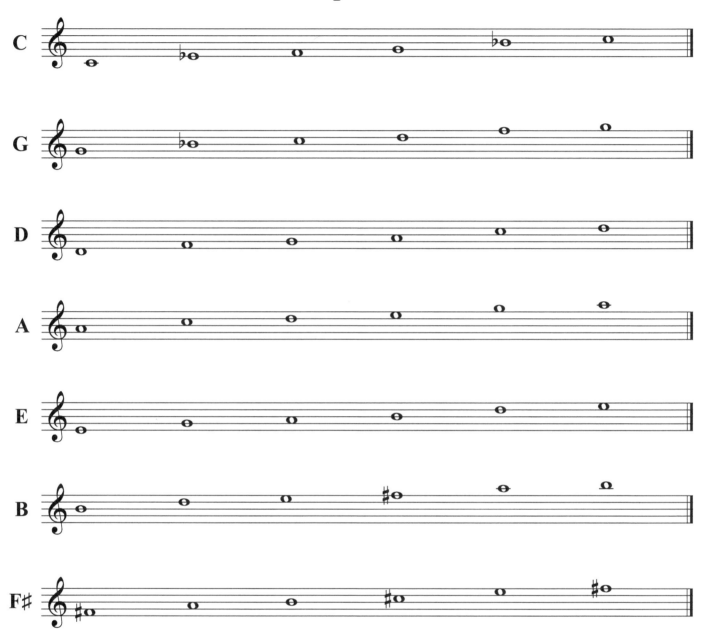

Blues minor pentatonic

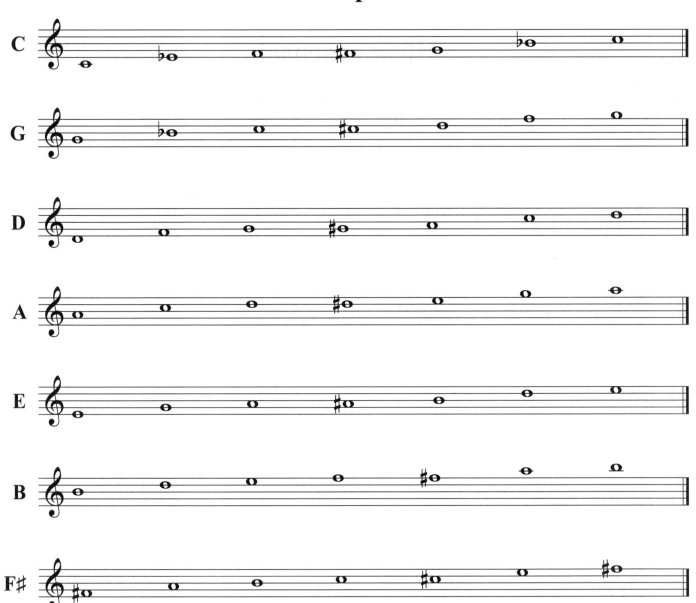

6. Features of Jazz Music

Swing is a jazz rhythmic pattern in which the first of each pair of notes played is extended and the second is shortened.

A triplet-like feel emerges in jazz rhythm. In a triplet, it is important to feel the first beat and accentuate the weaker (third) beat. With swing, a sense of anticipation and subsequent forward motion is created. You can develop your feeling for the beat by playing eighth note triplets through the beats of the measures.

Clap the rhythm while keeping the accents on the weak beat and counting triplets for each quarter. Keep them even.

1. Clap and count, accenting every first eighth note in each triplet.

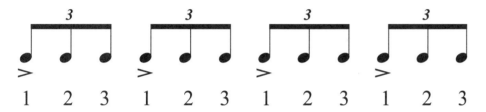

2. Clap and count. Now move the accent from the first eighth (in each triplet group) to the third.

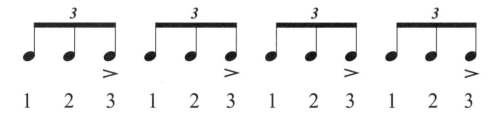

3. Clap and count. The first two eighth notes are joined by a tie, meaning the second eighth note is no longer played and the third eighth note is played with the accent, but it's important to note that the first eighth is always played without the accent.

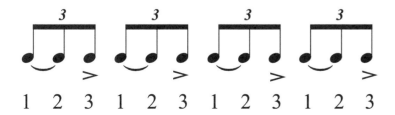

You can also have one quarter note instead of two tied notes.

The rhythm remains the same, but it looks different; clap through it one more time:

The rhythm in classical music is played as written, but in a jazz rhythmic pattern, the first eighth is extended and the second eighth is shortened and emphasized.

To make it easier to write down, the regular rhythm is usually written down on the sheet, and the eighths are not combined into triplet groups.

A notation usually is made above the treble clef, indicating that it is to be played in Swing style.

Therefore, if it is written like this:

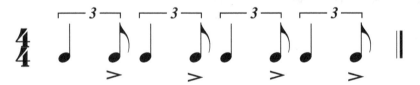

This rhythm pattern should be played like this:

If Swing is represented as a dotted eighth note and a sixteenth note, we'll get the familiar dotted rhythm.

Swing is the natural accentuation of a melody based on the relationship between felt and real rhythms and with continuous rhythmic movement.

Play with swing, the second eighth accented note is played shorter than the first note. Listen to the audio example:

C major

E blues minor pentatonic

E   G   A   A   B♭   B   D   E   E   G   A   A   B♭   B   D   E

Now let's play a minor pentatonic and a blues minor pentatonic with a swing. Listen to the audio example:

Pages 141-142

G minor pentatonic

G   B♭   C   D   F   G   G   F   D   C   B♭   G

G blues minor pentatonic

G   B♭   C   C#   D   F   G   G   F   D   C#   C   B♭   G

A minor pentatonic

A   C   D   E   G   A   A   G   E   D   C   A

A blues minor pentatonic

E minor pentatonic

E blues minor pentatonic

B minor pentatonic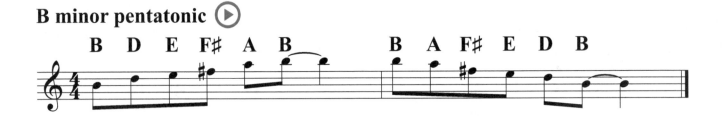

B blues minor pentatonic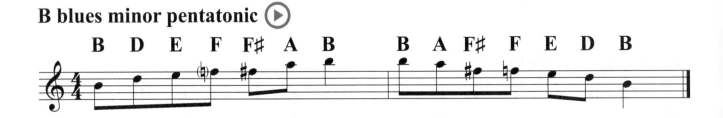

7. Grace Notes and Mordent

Grace or crushed notes (i.e., notes of very short duration) are an authentic and vital element in blues styles.

A grace note is an embellishment, an added note to the main note, which, therefore does not need to be emphasized.

The finesse and ease of the musical ornamentation is achieved when the finger movements are free and relaxed. There is also a contrast in dynamics (or volume) between the main melody tone and the musical embellishments that accompany it. This is done through contrasting changes in performer's blowing. All the while, rhythmic accuracy must be preserved.

Listen to the audio example for the exercise and practice playing it.

Pages 143-144 (4)

Now let's add grace notes to a blues tune. Listen to and *Page 144 - Exercise* play this exercise, then play it following the rhythm pattern in the audio.

Exercise

Avgusta Udartseva

Some Aspects of Articulation in Jazz

Legato

In classical music, the legato stroke is played without tongue involvement. In jazz music, legato without tongue involvement is used to join two or three eighth notes. Of course, legato without tongue use can be used in jazz for fast scale runs.

In jazz, when playing a phrase in which all the notes must be slurred together, a soft tongue attack is used, that is, the tongue is relaxed and round, as when pronouncing the syllable "Doo" and just barely touches the saxophone reed.

Non Legato

If there are no markings in the sheet music, all the ends of phrases should be played short by default, using the tongue, i.e. short notes are "plugged" with the tongue, which allows you to make a sharp sound end without sound decay.

Mordent

A mordent is a musical ornament that consists of a rapid single alternation of a note with the note above or below.

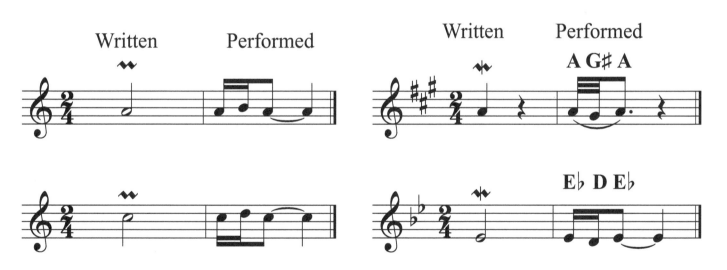

Exercise ▶

Avgusta Udartseva

8. Improvisation - First Steps

There are main tones in a regular scale or in a pentatonic scale around which the melodic line moves. The major tones in a scale or pentatonic are the first and fifth degrees. In the A minor pentatonic scale, these are the A and E notes:

A minor pentatonic

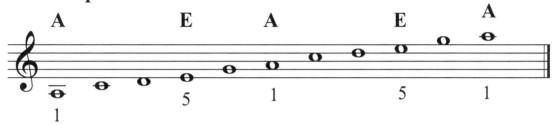

They form a kind of "backbone" of the melody, which forms the melody base. The auxiliary, secondary tones that fill the space between the main tones are, then, what makes up the "muscles" of the melodic line.

When creating a melody, we move around the main tones, connecting them with the help of the secondary tones.

Let's play a "swing" down from the main note:

Now let's play a "swing" upward from the main note:

Now play a down-and-up "long swing" rising - falling:

Now let's play up and down:

Now go down and then skip straight to the top note and back to the bottom note:

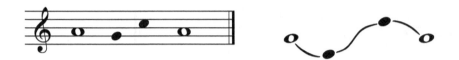

Now up and skip straight to the bottom note and return to the base note:

Now the movement will have an amplitude of two moves per note within the pentatonic down or up:

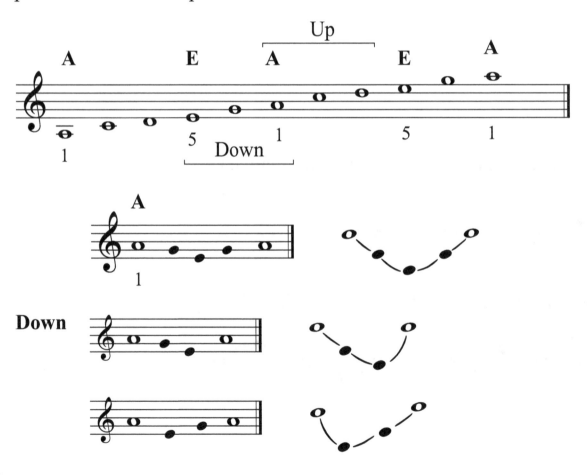

148

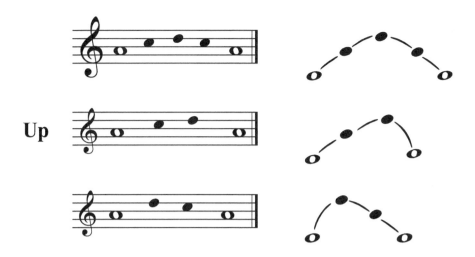

Up

Now try from the fifth degree (E note) to play all of the above moves.

Here's what you might get if you follow the above patterns for building a melody. Listen to and play this blues. Then play this blues with accompaniment.

Page 150

Blues in A minor

Avgusta Udartseva

In this blues in A minor, the movement of the melody is very simple. You can make up your own melody using the A minor pentatonic. Play along with the accompaniment to this blues.

Practice! It probably won't work right away, but the main thing is to be confident and know what key you're in.

Start by playing from the A note with a swing and adding grace notes to some notes. Play only a few grace notes at first, you need to build up confidence and then add a few more grace notes. A musical idea is first born in the mind and then spoken with the help of the instrument. The key is to know the notes of the A minor pentatonic.

Over time, you will gain more confidence and you will be able to make your improvisation more complex by adding more elaborate elements in terms of rhythm and melody.

9. Blues Square

A blues square is a verse that consists of three lines, each line consisting of two two-bar phrases that form a "question" and an "answer".

Question		Answer		
I (T)		**I** (T)		

Question		Answer		
IV (S)		**I** (T)		

Question		Answer		
V (D)	**IV** (S)	**I** (T)	**V** (D)	

The standard number of bars in the blues is 12. You can write 3 lines on paper, each line having 4 bars. This way it will be easier to navigate the music and you will have a good feel for the blues form.

The blues is built according to this pattern. You can practice it in the key you are comfortable with. It is important to feel the rhythm pulsation, so that you do not get lost in the music and feel the whole of the musical piece. This is especially important if you are playing in a musical group, where each musician has a different task and the main common thread is the blues pattern.

Practice playing with accompaniment in the A minor blues pentatonic scale. Below is an accompaniment chart showing the main notes in each bar. Remember that your improvisation will start with two and three notes.

Page 152

A - I (Tonic);   D - IV (Subdominant);   E - V (Dominant)

You will hear 2 versions of the accompaniment: the first is 12 bars, the second is 24 bars (12+12). One audio file is for saxophones in E♭ and the other is for the saxophone in B♭ ▶. Improvising and playing by ear is not as difficult as many people think. We improvise on two notes, then on three notes, then on four notes. At the same time, be sure not to lose the fun of it all.

Two-Bar Rhythmic Patterns are examples that can be used as basic rhythmic structures for improvisation or composition. Listen to them and play through them.

Two-Bars Rhythmic Patterns ▶

Page 153

153

Here is another example of blues in D minor. Listen to it and play through it.

Blues in D minor

Avgusta Udartseva

Now, try to play your own melody along with the accompaniment for this blues (turn on the audio track that has no saxophone playing with it).

From Simple to Complex

It is very important to follow this principle: first learn to take one or two notes so that you can focus on the sound and feel good when playing. Then you expand the range and create more complex runs.

Don't be disappointed if you don't get your improvisation right the first time through. You need time to learn to feel the rhythm. Just three notes are enough for the melody itself to begin to form in your hands. And when there is added excitement and joy, you will feel like you've got wings! This intense feeling will motivate you to continue to grow in this fascinating direction.

The courage, confidence and good mood should always accompany you when you play your instrument!

DON'T FORGET! You should always play with a quality tone. A quality tone is not that difficult to achieve if you play just one or two notes.

Practice Time

The most important thing is consistency and repetition. Do your best to practice every day, even if you can only play for 15 minutes.

If you don't have much time to practice in a day, do a short warm-up in the form of a minimal set of exercises, and the rest of the time play what you like - your favorite songs or improvisation. Don't forget to play with a metronome, it will help you in the future to play with any accompaniment without getting lost.

The minimum full lesson time is one hour. The time is distributed as follows: half of the time you practice your technique, and the other half you spend working on your pieces and improvisation. Working on the technique should be practiced in the following sequence: 1 - work on the tone, 2 - scales, 4 - pentatonics, 5 - arpeggios.

It is very useful to work on technical stuff (scales, arpeggios) silently - it trains fingers, helps master fingering and inner hearing. Such exercises can be done at almost any time of day. You can also combine them with watching interesting movies, for example! In addition, even without your instrument you can practice by mentally visualizing the fingering and moving your fingers. That helps a lot, especially if you were traveling, as an example.

10. Vibrato

Vibrato breathes life into the sound of the saxophone bringing it closer to the human voice and making the sound more natural and supple.

A good vibrato is essentially a change (pulsation) in pitch, usually accompanied by a pulsation in volume to a degree that adds a certain silkiness, tenderness and richness to the tone.

Once you have sufficiently developed a confident and even tone, a stable and even airflow, you will want to learn how to add a nice vibrato to your saxophone playing.

Vibrato is a technique that allows you to emphasize the melody, adds expressiveness to the tone, as well as accentuate main culminations in your performance.

Vibrato is very often used by saxophonists in all musical styles and genres. It makes you literally feel the shape of the sound wave. When using vibrato, the sound becomes palpable, as if you witnessed a two-dimensional, flat picture transform into a three-dimensional graphic.

Physical Characteristics of Vibrato

Technically, vibrato is a slight change in dynamics and pitch with a specific amplitude and repetition rate of that change.

The extent to which we change the dynamics and pitch at the peak is the amplitude and can be represented as a vertical line, while the repetition rate of the amplitude can be represented horizontally.

These two parameters of vibrato we can mix at our discretion:
1. High amplitude + frequent repetition
2. High amplitude + slow repetition
3. Low amplitude + frequent repetition
4. Low amplitude + slow repetition

The rate of your vibrato should remain relatively constant at all dynamic levels and in all registers, but nevertheless, the width or amplitude of the vibrato will inevitably change with the change in volume.

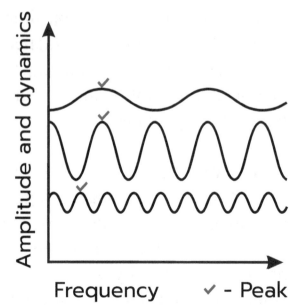

156

Vibrato Technique

Vibrato is produced by changing the length and density of the air column. For a quality and well-controlled vibrato, you must have **the correct performing breathing.**

We can distinguish two ways of playing vibrato - upper and lower. Upper - with the help of the embouchure (mouth muscles) and lower - with the help of your diaphragm.

The most common way to play saxophone vibrato is to move your jaw down and then up, as if saying "wah-wah".

It is important not to clamp the reed with your lip and to keep a good air supply!

This movement of the jaw will be almost invisible visually and is produced as a result of the interaction of the airflow with the reed. There is a slight change in the pitch of the underlying tone.

1. First you need to get a good basic tone with good airflow. Then practice changing the tone with the lower lip. Play the G note confidently and smoothly.

No vibrato

G ────────────────────────────

2. Now play just one sound with pitch change, slowly saying the syllable "wah-wah."

Slow vibrato with good breathing

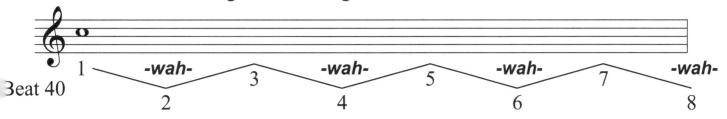

3. Now begin doing the vibrato, starting with one wave change on the sound, for one beat of the metronome at a slow pace (40 beats per minute and then go up to 70 beats per minute).

1 pulse per beat

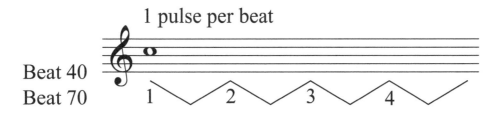

157

4. Practice vibrato starting with three wave changes on the sound, for one beat of the metronome at a slow tempo (50 beats per minute and then go up to 80 beats per minute). A simple solution is to say three "wahs" per quarter note.

3 pulses per beat

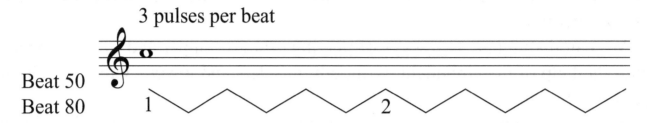

Now the speed of vibrato is moving to four wave changes (or "wah") per quarter note. The speed is 80 beats per minute. This is an adequate vibrato speed, but the performer can use it as a reference point from which a faster or slower vibrato sound can be created from time to time. Sometimes it will be difficult for an inexperienced player to produce four waves.

4 pulses per beat

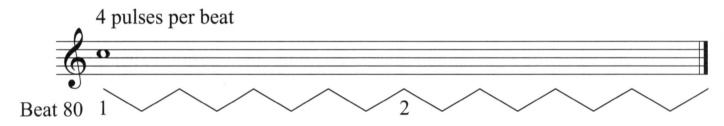

At this point, it is crucial that the airflow remains constant; remember to supply plenty of air when adding vibrato to a good basic "straight" sound.

Practice Turning Vibrato "On" and "Off"

Using a metronome set to 80 beats per minute, select a sustained mezzo-forte (moderately loud) pitch in the middle register, perhaps a G or F note in the first octave.

Play four beats without vibrato and then four beats with vibrato for four bars; do not articulate (no tongue use) except to start the sustained pitch. Listen carefully to make sure that the quality of the basic sound does not change with the addition of vibrato.

Continue the exercise in the reverse order: start with vibrato for four counts, and then play four fractions without vibrato. Later, as you get better at it, you should use other registers and other dynamic levels.

This vibrato is fairly easy to adjust in amplitude and frequency, but it will be erratic and unstable in the absence of a strong and even exhalation.

You need to practice playing long sounds every day or do several 15-minute approaches a day. You don't need to disassemble the instrument every time, just try to play long sounds, getting even breathing and free (but not sluggish) position of the embouchure. At first, the "wah-wah" will give you an idea of how the sound should change, swinging evenly and deviating slightly from the main note.

Ideally, you should come to a technique where the sound is produced by the interaction of the airflow with the reed. When you master that, you won't need to put additional lower lip pressure on the reed.

Vibrato occurs as a result of:

1. Changes in the length and density of the column of air flowing from your lungs to the saxophone.

2. Changes in the angle of attack of the airflow that contacts the reed.

Movements of the upper palate and the base of the tongue together with the movement of the lower jaw change the length of the air column and the direction of the airflow.

When it is Better to Use Vibrato

First you should get a good basic "straight" sound. Only then you can move to practicing the vibrato technique. It is important to note that vibrato should not be used on every note. It can enrich and enhance a good basic tone, but it can also be inappropriate and should therefore be used sparingly.

The best way to learn vibrato is through imitation. Many students become familiar with vibrato by listening carefully to the good tone of their teacher's saxophone. Listen to the manner of playing of different fine saxophonists in audio recordings, as everyone has their own unique sound, their own way of playing, their own improvisation technique, their own vibrato!

Important: To learn how to play vibrato on a saxophone, you need to remember the following:

Watch the video

Vibrato technique

- A good vibrato should feel natural and effortless.
- The vibrato (vibration of the sound) should not distort the main note too much.
- The vibrato should be rhythmic, ideally with an acceleration from a slower (wider) swing of the sound to a faster swing.
- When performing vibrato, use not only the movement of the lower lip, but also your breathing, since it greatly affects the intensity of the reed's oscillation.

Chapter 3
Part 2 ▶

Pages 183-217
Chapter 3 - Part 2
Songs with Accompaniment

For any questions, comments or suggestions, email us at:
avgustaudartseva@gmail.com

Fascinating Rhythm

music by George Gershwin
lyrics by Ira Gershwin

Moderato

Got a lit-tle rhy-thm, A rhy-thm, a rhy-thm

That pi - ta-pats through my brain.

So darn per-sis-tent, The day is-n't dis-tant

When it - 'll drive me in - sane.

Comes in the mor - ning Wi - thout a - ny war - ning

And hangs a - round all day.

I'll have to sneak up to it, Some-day, and speak up to it

15
I hope it lis - tens when I say:

Refrain

17
"Fas - ci - na - ting Rhy - thm You've got me on the go! Fas - ci -

19
na - ting Rhy - thm I'm all a - qui - ver.

21
What a mess you're ma - king! The neigh - bours want to know why I'm

23
al - ways sha - king Just like a fli - ver.

25
Each mor - ning I get up with the sun,

28
(Stars a hop - ping ne - ver stop - ping) To find at

30
night, no work has been done. I know that

That's an Irish Lullaby

James Royce Shannon

Moderato

O - ver in Kil - lar - ney, Ma - ny years a -
go, Me Mi - ther sang a song to me In
tones so sweet and low, Just a sim - ple lit - tle
dit - ty, In her good ould I - rish way, And I'd
give the world if she could sing That song to me this day.

Refrain

"Too - ra - loo - ra - loo - ral, Too - ra - loo - ra -
li, Too - ra - loo - ra - loo - ral,

I'll See You in My Dreams

music by Isham Jones
lyrics by Gus Kahn

Moderato

Tho' the days are long, Twi - light sings a song,
In the drea - ry gray; Of an - oth - er day,

Or the hap - pi - ness that used to be,
You'll be far - a - way and it be blue;

Soon my eyes will close, Soon I'll find re - pose,
Still I hope and pray, Thru each wear - y day,

And in dreams you're al - ways near to me. I'll
For it brings the night and dreams of you.

see you in my dreams Hold you

in my dreams, Some - one took you

out of my arms, Still I feel the thrill of your charms

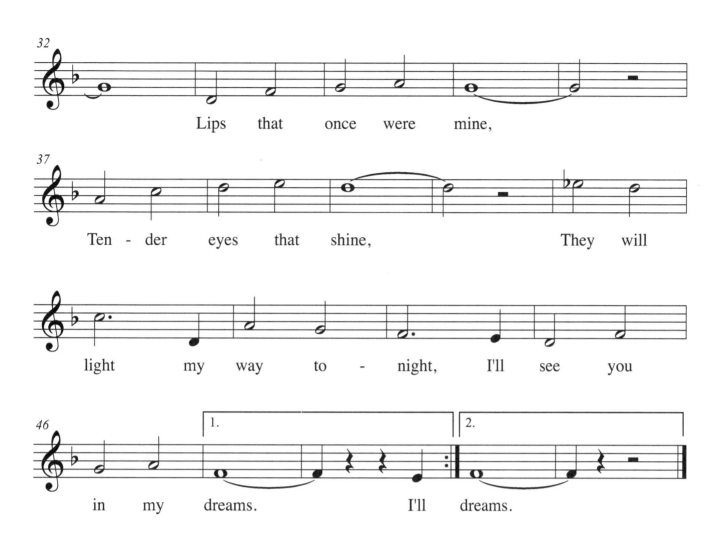

Limehouse Blues

Philip Braham

Allegro moderato

170

171

Sugar Blues

music by Clarence Williams
lyrics by Lucy Fletcher

lo - vin man's sweet as he can be, but the

dog - gone fool turned so-ur on me. I'm so un-hap-py, I

feel so bad, I could lay me down and die. You can

say what you choose but I'm all con - fused, I've

got the sweet, sweet su - gar blues, more su - gar, I've

1.
2.
got the sweet, sweet su - gar blues. I've goy the // blues.

Till We Meet Again

music by Richard A. Whiting
lyrics by Raymond B. Egan

Adagio

There's a song in the land of the li - ly

Each sweet - heart has heard with a sigh

O - ver high gar - den walls This sweet e - cho

falls As a sol - dier boy whis - pers good - bye

Smile the while you kiss me sad a -

dieu. When the cloud roll by I'll come to

you Then the skies will seem more

blue   Down   in   lov   -   ers   lane   my

dear   -   ie   Wed   -   ding   bells   will   ring   so   mer - ri -

ly   Ev   -   'ry   tear   will   be   a   mem - o -

ry   So   wait   and   pray   each   night   for

me.   Till   we   meet   a - gain.   gain

The Saint Louis Blues

W. C. Handy

I hate to see that eve-nin' sun go down,

I hate to see that eve-nin' sun go down.

It makes me think I'm on my last go 'round.

Fee-lin' to-mor-row just like I feel to-day,

Fee-lin' to-mor-row just like I feel to-day,

I'll pack my grip and make my ge-ta-way. St. Lou-is

wo-man with her dia-mond rings, Pulls that man

a-round   by her ap-ron   strings.   Wasn't the

pow-der   and the store - bought   hair   The man

I love   wouldn't go   no - where, no - where.   The man

Got the   St. Lou - is blues, just as   blue as   I   can be.

He has   got   a heart like a rock   cast   in   the sea.

Or_   else   he   wouldn't   have   gone

so   far   from   me.

My Little Dream Girl

music by Anatol Friedland
lyrics by Louis Wolfe Gilbert

Beale Street Blues

W. C. Handy

New Je - ru - sa - lem. I'd rath - er be here, _____ than an-y place I

know I'd rath - er be here _____

than an - y place I know It's goin' to

take the Ser - gant For to make me go, _____

_____ Goin' to the ri - ver, _____ may - be, bye and

bye Goin' to the ri - ver, _____

and there's a rea - son why Be - cause the

ri - ver's wet ___ And Beale Street's done gone dry.

Clap Yo' Hands

music by George Gershwin
lyrics by Ira Gershwin

Clap - a yo' hand!   Slap - a yo' thigh!   Hal - le-lu - yah! Hal - le-

lu - yah! Ev - 'ry-bo - dy come a - long and join the ju-bi -

lee!   On the sands of time you are on-ly a

peb-ble;   Re - mem - ber, trou - ble must be

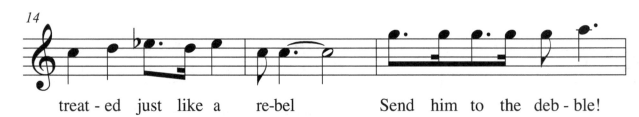

treat - ed just like a re-bel   Send him to the deb - ble!

Clap - a yo' hand!   Slap - a yo' thigh!   Hal - le-lu - yah! Hal - le-

lu-yah! Ev-'ry-bo-dy come a-long and join the ju-bi lee!

Songs with Accompaniment

Aloha 'Oe

Lili'uokalani

Let Him Go, Let Him Tarry

Traditional Irish

Now Brid-get was a Col-leen with an
in-de-pen-dent air, And Brid-get had a sweet-heart who was
gay and de-bon-air, He would woo her, court her jilt her near-ly
ev-ry oth-er day, Till fi-nal-ly Miss Brid-get was
heard, at last to say. Let him go, ler him tar-ry, let him
sink, or let him swim, He does-n't care for me, And
I don't care for him, He can go and get an-oth-er, That I

hope he will en - joy. For I'm goin' to - mar - ry A

far nic - er boy. Let him go, let him

go. Let him go, let him tar - ry, let him

stay, He can go, and get an - oth - er That I

hope he will en - joy, For I'm going to mar - ry A

far nic - er boy
1.
2.
Let him boy.

Page 184

185

Ja-Da

Bob Carleton

Swing!

Ja-da   Ja-da   Ja-da Ja-da Jing, Jing,

Jing.   Ja - da   Ja - da

Ja - da   Ja - da   Jing,   Jing,_____   Jing.

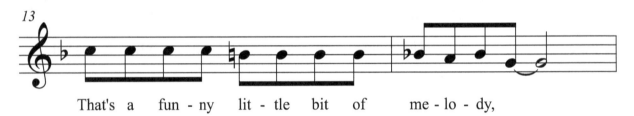

That's a   fun - ny   lit - tle   bit   of   me - lo - dy,

It's   so   soo - thing and ap - peal - ling to   me,   It goes

Ja - da   Ja - da   Ja - da Ja - da Jing, Jing,

Jing, Oh yeah!   Ja - da Ja - da Jing, Jing,   Jing!

Down in the Valley

American folk song

Adagio

Down in the Val - ley, Val - ley so

low, _____ Hang your head ov -

er, hear the wind blow. _____

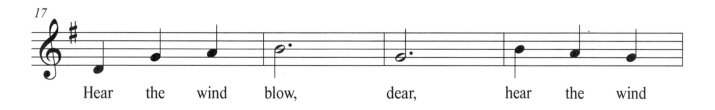

Hear the wind blow, dear, hear the wind

blow, _____ Hang you head ov -

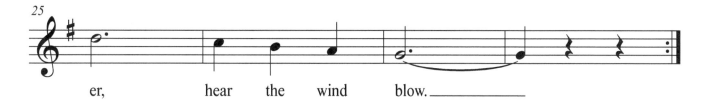

er, hear the wind blow. _____

Page 187

187

All by Myself

Irving Berlin

Moderato

I'm so un-hap-py What-'ll I do, I long for

some-bo-dy who, will sym-pa-thize with me; I'm

grow-ing so tired of liv-ing a-lone, I lie a-

wake all night and cry - No-bo-dy loves me that's why.

All by my-self in the morn - ing

All by my-self in the night;

I sit a-lone in a co-sy Mor-ris chair,

So un-hap-py there   Play-ing sol-i-taire

All   by my-self   I get lone - ly

Watch - ing the clock   on the shelf   I'd love to

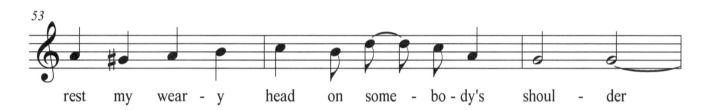

rest my wear - y   head   on some-bo-dy's   shoul - der

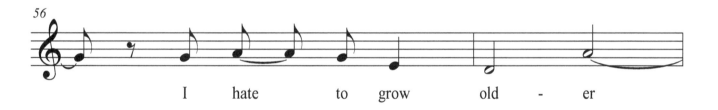

I   hate   to   grow   old - er

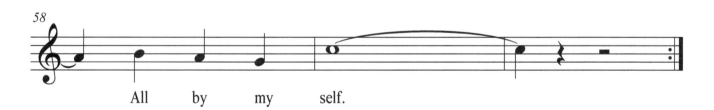

All   by   my   self.

Page 188

Wade in the Water

Traditional song

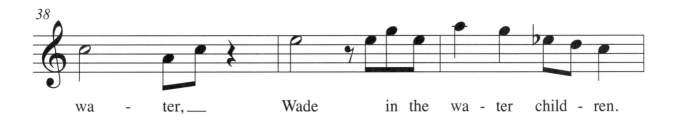

Wade   in the

wa - ter,___   Wade   in the wa - ter child - ren.

Wade in the wa - ter   God's gonna trouble the wa - ter.

Page 190

191

The Man I Love ▶

George Gershwin

Amazing Grace

Traditional song

The Birth of the Blues

music by Ray Henderson
lyrics by Buddy DeSylva
and Lew Brown

jail came the wail Of a down heart-ed frail,

And they played that As part of the

blues From a whip-poor will Out on a hill,

They took a new note, Pushed it through a

horn 'Til it was worn In-to a blue note!

And then they nursed it, re-hearsed it, And gave

out the news That the South-land

gave birth to the blues!

After You've Gone

music by Turner Layton
lyrics by Henry Creamer

Now won't you list-en hon-ey while I say——

How could you tell me that you're going a - way—— Don't say that

we must part—— Don't break your ba-by's heart You know I've loved you for these

man-y years Loved you night and day——

Oh hon-ey ba - by cant you see my tears—— List-en while I

say—— Af - ter you've gone and left me cry-ing

Af - ter you've gone There's no de-ny-ing, you'll feel blue,

You'll feel sad, You'll miss the best-est pal you've ev - er had——

There'll come a time, now don't for-get it, There'll come a time,

when you'll re - gret it Oh! Babe, Think what you're do - ing

you know my love for you will drive me to ru - in, Af - ter you've gone

Af - ter you've gone a - way,_____ a - way.

Watch the video

After You've Gone

Page 196

Swanee

music by George Gershwin
lyrics by Irving Caesar

Presto

I've been a - way from you a long time

I ne - ver thought I'd miss you so___

Some - how I felt   Your   love was real

Near   you   I long to   be,

The birds are   sin - ging It is   song - time,

The ban - jos strum - min' soft and   low,___

I   know that   you   Yearn   for me   too;

Swa - nee   You're cal - ling___

Swa   - nee   How I love you How I love you

My   dear old   Swa - nee;   I'd give the

Can't Help Lovin' Dat Man

music by Jerome Kern
lyrics by Oscar Hammerstein II

All Alone

Irving Berlin

Allegro

Just like a mel-o-dy that lin - gers on,

You seem to haunt me night and day

I nev - er re - al - ized till you had gone

How much I cared a - bout you, I can't live with-out you.

All a - lone i'm so all a - lone There is

no one else but you.

All a - lone by the tel - e - phone wait - ing

Page 202

Tea for Two

Vincent Youmans

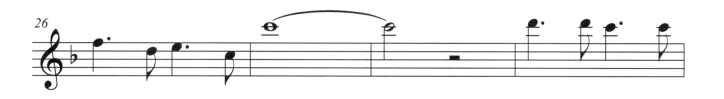

 Page 204

Take Me Out to the Ball Game

music by Albert Von Tilzer
lyrics by Jack Norworth

Oh, Lady Be Good!

music by George Gershwin
lyrics by Ira Gershwin

Page 208

Sweet Georgia Brown

music by Ben Bernie and
Maceo Pinkard
lyrics by Kenneth Casey

No gal made ___ has got a shade On

Sweet Geor-gia Brown ___ Two left feel ___ but oh so neat ___ has

Sweet Geor-gia Brown ___ They all sigh ___ and wan-na die ___ For

Sweet Geor-gia Brown I'll tell - you just why ___ you know I don't

lie Not much! It's been said ___ she knocks-'em dead ___ when

she lands in town ___ Since she came ___ why it's a shame how

she cools' em down ___ Fel - lers she can't get ___ are

fel - lers she ain't met ___ Geor-gia claimed her

Geor-gia named her Sweet Geor-gia Brown ___

Let My People Go

Negro spiritual

When Is - rael was in E - gypt land, ___ Let my peo-ple go,
need not al - ways weep and mourn,

___ Op - pressed so hard they could not stand,
And wear these slav - 'ry chains for - lorn,

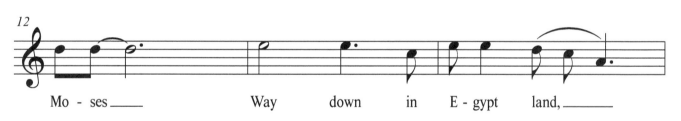

Let my peo - ple go, ___ Go down ___

Mo - ses ___ Way down in E - gypt land, ___

1.
2.

Tell old ___ Pha - raoh, Let my peo-ple go. ___ We

Page 211

211

Hello! Ma Baby

Howard and Emerson

Moderato

I've got a lit-tle ba-by, but she's out of sight, I

talk to her a-cross the tel-e-phone; ___ I've nev-er seen my hon-ey but she's

mine all right; So take my tip and leave this gal a-lone. ___

Ev-'ry sin-gle morn-ing, you will hear me yell, "Hey Cen-tral! fix me up a-long the

line." ___ He con-nects me with ma hon-ey, then I rings the bell, And

this is what I say to ba-by mine, ___ Hel-lo! ma ba-by,

Hel-lo! ma hon-ey, Hel-lo! ma rag-time gal, ___

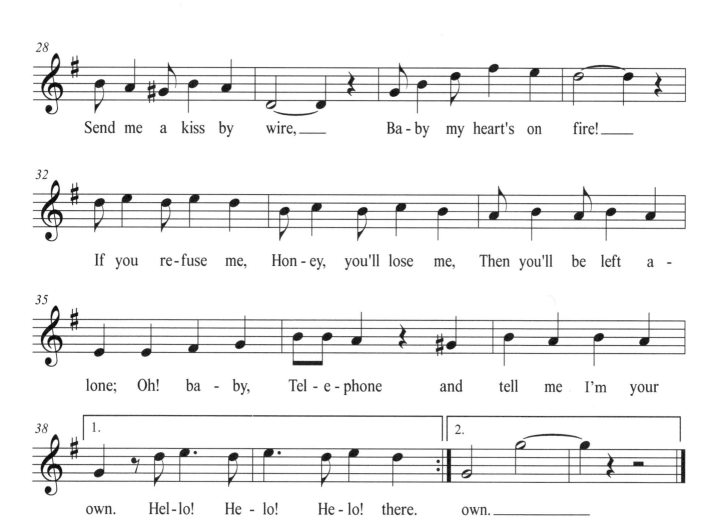

Send me a kiss by wire,___ Ba - by my heart's on fire!___

If you re-fuse me, Hon - ey, you'll lose me, Then you'll be left a -

lone; Oh! ba - by, Tel - e - phone and tell me I'm your

1. own. Hel-lo! He - lo! He - lo! there. 2. own._____

Page 212

In the Good Old Summer Time

music by George Evans
lyrics by Ren Shields

time.   In the good old sum - mer time,   In the

good old sum - mer time,   Strol - ling thro' the sha - dy

lanes,   With your ba - by mine;   You hold her hand and

she holds yours. And that's a ve - ry good sign   That

she's your toot - sey woot - sey in The good old

sum - mer time.   In the   time.

Page 214

215

Lyrical Melody

Avgusta Udartseva

Andante

The Way Home ▶

Avgusta Udartseva

Andante

The major scales

W - Whole step
H - Half step

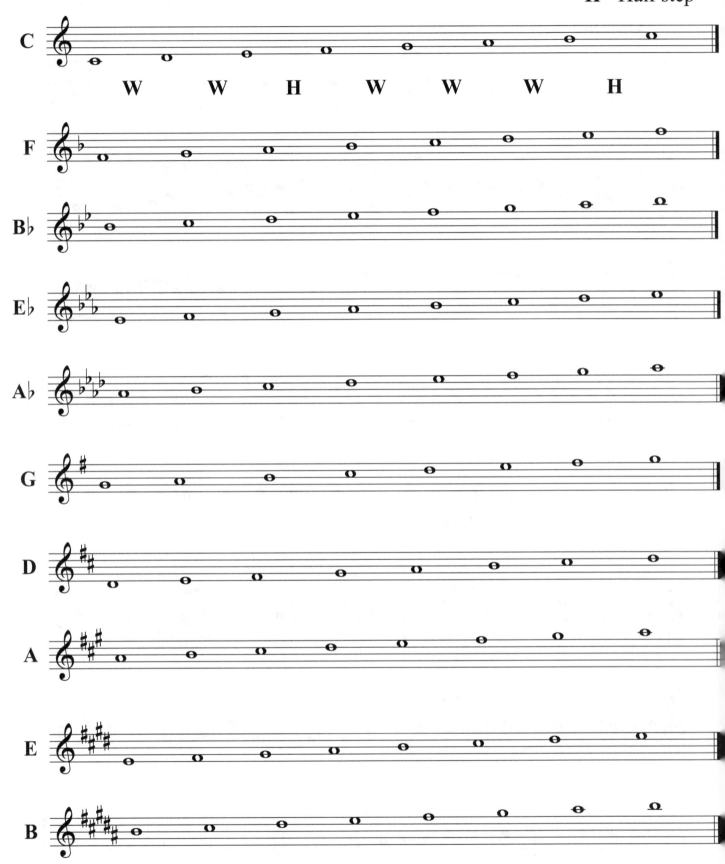

218

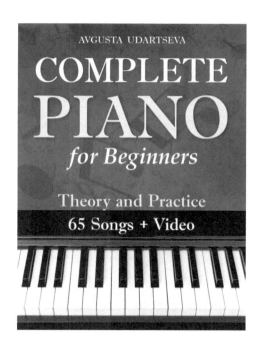

ISBN: 979-8361128570

ASIN: B0BKYHL7PC

Learning to play your favorite songs on the piano is easy!

Today the piano is probably the most popular musical instrument in the world. Playing this instrument will give you an unforgettable experience.

The book contains musical theory, practical exercises, and 65 popular songs for adults.

United States   **United Kingdom**   **Canada**

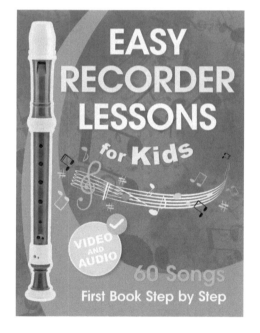

ISBN: 979-8386419004

ASIN: B0BXMX7ZVN

- Learning step by step: starting with more simple tunes, then gradually moving to more complex songs;
- Includes music theory, instrument history, practice, recommendations and many entertaining songs;
- Learn the position of the body and hands, how to breathe properly and play easily;
- Letters above each note and simple explanations;
- Convenient large US Letter print size;
- Video accompaniment to all lessons by direct link inside the book;
- 2-in-1 Book: Recorder lessons and video + 60 Songs.

And it's great for adults

United States   **United Kingdom**   **Canada**

Made in United States
Troutdale, OR
09/27/2024

23200004R00124